Cloud Computing

OTHER TITLES IN THE TECHNOLOGY 360 SERIES:

TECHNOLOGY 360

Cloud Computing

BY ANDREW A. KLING

LUCENT BOOKS
A part of Gale, Cengage Learning

GALE
CENGAGE Learning·

Farmington Hills, Mich • San Francisco • New York • Waterville, Maine
Meriden, Conn • Mason, Ohio • Chicago

LIBRARY OF CONGRESS CATALOGING-IN-PUBLICATION DATA

Kling, Andrew A., 1961-
  Cloud computing / by Andrew A. Kling.
    pages cm -- (Technology 360)
  Includes bibliographical references and index.
  ISBN 978-1-4205-1158-1 (hardcover)
  1. Cloud computing--Juvenile literature. I. Title.
  QA76.585.K57 2014
  004.67'82--dc23
                        2014003441

Lucent Books
27500 Drake Rd
Farmington Hills MI 48331

ISBN-13: 978-1-4205-1158-1
ISBN-10: 1-4205-1158-0

Printed in the United States of America
1 2 3 4 5 6 7 18 17 16 15 14

CONTENTS

FOREWORD

"As we go forward, I hope we're going to continue to use technology to make really big differences in how people live and work."
—Sergey Brin, co-founder of Google

The past few decades have seen some amazing advances in technology. Many of these changes have had a direct and measureable impact on the way people live, work, and play. Communication tools, such as cell phones, satellites, and the Internet, allow people to keep in constant contact across longer distances and from the most remote places. In fields related to medicine, existing technologies—digital imaging devices, robotics, and lasers, for example—are being used to redefine surgical procedures and diagnostic techniques. As technology has become more complex, however, so have the related ethical, legal, and safety issues.

Psychologist B.F. Skinner once noted that "the real problem is not whether machines think but whether men do." Recent advances in technology have, in many cases, drastically changed the way people view the world around them. They can have a conversation with someone across the globe at lightning speed, access a huge universe of information with the click of a key, or become an avatar in a virtual world of their own making. While advances like these have been viewed as a great boon in some quarters, they have also opened the door to questions about whether or not the speed of technological advancement has come at an unspoken price. A closer examination of the evolution and use of these devices provides a deeper understanding of the social, cultural, and ethical implications that they may hold for our future.

Technology 360 not only explores how evolving technologies work, but also examines the short- and long-term impact of their use on society as a whole. Each volume in Technology 360 focuses on a particular invention, device, or family of similar devices, exploring how the device was developed; how it works; its impact on society; and possible future uses. Volumes also contain a timeline specific to each topic, a glossary of technical terms used in the text, and a subject index. Sidebars, photos and detailed illustrations, tables, charts and graphs help further illuminate the text.

Titles in this series emphasize inventions and devices familiar to most readers, such as robotics, digital cameras, iPods, and video games. Not only will users get an easy-to-understand, "nuts and bolts" overview of these inventions, they will also learn just how much these devices have evolved. For example, in 1973 a Motorola cell phone weighed about 2 pounds (.907kg) and cost $4,000—today, cell phones weigh only a few ounces and are inexpensive enough for every member of the family to have one. Lasers— long a staple of the industrial world—have become highly effective surgical tools, capable of reshaping the cornea of the eye and cleaning clogged arteries. Early video games were played on large machines in arcades; now, many families play games on sophisticated home systems that allow for multiple players and cross-location networking.

IMPORTANT DATES IN THE DEVELOPMENT

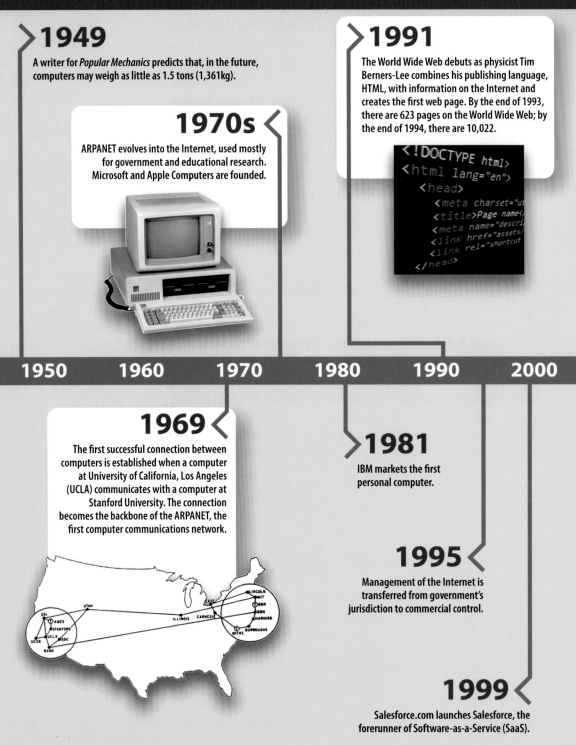

1949
A writer for *Popular Mechanics* predicts that, in the future, computers may weigh as little as 1.5 tons (1,361kg).

1970s
ARPANET evolves into the Internet, used mostly for government and educational research. Microsoft and Apple Computers are founded.

1991
The World Wide Web debuts as physicist Tim Berners-Lee combines his publishing language, HTML, with information on the Internet and creates the first web page. By the end of 1993, there are 623 pages on the World Wide Web; by the end of 1994, there are 10,022.

1950   1960   1970   1980   1990   2000

1969
The first successful connection between computers is established when a computer at University of California, Los Angeles (UCLA) communicates with a computer at Stanford University. The connection becomes the backbone of the ARPANET, the first computer communications network.

1981
IBM markets the first personal computer.

1995
Management of the Internet is transferred from government's jurisdiction to commercial control.

1999
Salesforce.com launches Salesforce, the forerunner of Software-as-a-Service (SaaS).

OF CLOUD COMPUTING

2010

Rackspace Hosting and NASA create an open-source cloud computing operating system called OpenStack, designed to compete with other systems from companies such as Amazon and Microsoft.

2001

SaaS makes its first appearance in technology literature.

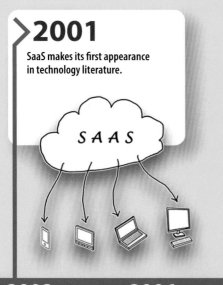

2013

In April, streaming music site Pandora reaches 69 million users and streaming video site Netflix reaches 29 million users.

2002	2006	2010	2012	2013

2012

In December, the AWS data center in Northern Virginia suffers an outage that crashes Netflix for most of Christmas Eve.

2006

Google debuts Google Docs, a suite of office programs in SaaS.

2002

Amazon debuts the first offering of what becomes Amazon Web Services (AWS), called Simple Storage Service, or S3.

The Cloud Computing Revolution

The Western Maryland Research and Education Center (WMREC) is a branch of the University of Maryland Extension (UME), a statewide education system within the College of Agriculture and Natural Resources at the University of Maryland. For more than 150 years, UME has provided education and problem-solving assistance to Maryland communities and citizens. UME's university faculty and staff perform research into agricultural and natural resources sciences. They conduct experiments into growing fruit and grains, raising chickens and goats, and improving farmland ecology. They also provide practical advice for promoting woodland and habitat conservation and managing the spread of invasive species.

Additionally, the staff creates and presents educational outreach programs for the citizens of Maryland and the surrounding states. These programs are held at schools, universities, community centers, and parks, and provide an opportunity for the staff to receive feedback about their research efforts.

Sharing Research Through Education

Increasingly, the faculty and staff at WMREC rely on computers and the Internet to complete their research and outreach. For example, nutrient management specialist Heather Hutchinson creates and moderates online courses that demonstrate advanced techniques for managing farmland soil health. Her students create documents and take exams from their own computers, without ever stepping foot onto WMREC's facility.

A webinar (a combination of the terms *web* and *seminar*) is another popular method used at WMREC for sharing research information. For example, natural resources extension specialist Jonathan Kays presents experts from a variety of habitat conservation fields who share advice in techniques for managing woodland properties via the web. Sheep and goat specialist Susan Schoenian conducts an annual webinar series that educates about improving sheep and goat herds, with an emphasis on ensuring healthy offspring.

Kays, Schoenian, and others at the university use a program called Adobe Connect. Participants log on to a website and watch the experts guide them through the educational material. They have the ability to chat in real time with the presenters or fellow participants. The advantage of this program is that the participants need not download it or install any specialized software on their computer. They only need a high-speed Internet connection.

At the same time, other members of the WMREC community also use the Internet to communicate with family and colleagues. For example, at a lunchtime gathering, Dee Dee Allen, a regional administrative assistant, discussed her daughter's musical tastes and used her smartphone to access YouTube to share with her friends a favorite video of her youngster's.

Each of these examples takes advantage of the opportunities afforded by the World Wide Web to communicate and collaborate with individuals across the room, across the state, or around the world. Additionally, each of these takes advantage of a technology innovation called cloud computing.

Cloud Computing

Cloud computing is a technology that enables consumers, developers, and businesses to communicate and collaborate

Cloud-based technology allows businesses in different locations to collaborate and work in real time via a high-speed Internet connection.

by accessing software applications, data storage, and computing processing capacity over the Internet. In the world of the Internet, the cloud refers to the vast amount of information that computer users can access via the World Wide Web without the need for purchasing and installing specialized programs on their computers. Working in the cloud enables users to avoid storing information, programs, or files on their hard drives. They can take advantage of video development or accounting software, for instance, without having to download it, and they can access their personal data created with those programs numerous times without having to store it on their personal devices. Computer users are now accustomed to communicating and collaborating across the Internet with friends, family, and acquaintances; in doing so, they are often accessing information in the cloud. In this way, and often without realizing it, they are participating in cloud computing.

Cloud computing is similar to the advances in Internet applications known as Web 2.0. Like Web 2.0, cloud computing enables computer users to share their opinions and creativity through a variety of computer programs, independent of a computer operating system. Additionally, like Web 2.0, cloud computing is available on a wide range of devices, such as laptops, tablets, and smartphones. But there are a number of important differences between cloud computing and Web 2.0.

To understand the differences between cloud computing and Web 2.0, it is important to remember the distinction between the Internet and the World Wide Web. The Internet is a vast network of networks, the collection of interconnected computers, and everything that can be considered online, including e-mail, browsers, and the World Wide Web. The Web is just one application among many that uses the Internet, comprised of billions of sites and pages. One way to think of the relationship between the two is to imagine the Internet as a vast ocean and the Web as a massive fleet of ships and boats that enables people to navigate it.

While Web 2.0 is often seen as a way for individuals to participate in the World Wide Web, cloud computing plays an important role in commercial applications on the Internet. Cloud computing enables businesses to shift the burden of managing and maintaining computer hardware from their own staff to providers whose businesses specialize in these fields. Additionally, the rise of cloud computing is drawing comparisons to established utilities such as water, electricity, and natural gas services, which charge customers for what they use and which make these resources available to customers on demand. Similarly, cloud computing customers purchase services from providers, paying only for what they use, and have access to important resources on demand.

Cloud computing enables both the casual Internet user and the specialized programming developer to access information from around the world almost instantaneously. It is important to remember, however, that computers were once extremely rare and incredibly expensive, and access to them was restricted to a select few who understood their machine languages. It is in this era, in which equipment called mainframes and dumb terminals were used, that the story of cloud computing begins.

CHAPTER 1

From Mainframes to Servers

Cloud computing is the result of more than sixty years of research into computers. Today's twenty-first-century computers bear little resemblance to the earliest electronic devices bearing that label. Today's machines are compact and portable; the first machines were huge, taking up entire rooms within companies and universities.

These early computers used huge arrays of vacuum tubes and mechanical switches to create electrical circuits. They could perform only one task at a time but were capable of solving complex calculations such as determining artillery trajectories and breaking communications codes. They performed numbers calculations that had previously taken hours or days to complete using earlier techniques. Researchers, developers, and students realized that these machines represented a major step forward in working with information. The machines automated tasks that challenged and fatigued human workers such as accurately adding long columns of numbers, multiplying, and dividing. Equally important, the computers completed such tasks in a fraction of the time it took to do them manually.

Each new advancement in machine programming led to faster speeds and smaller size, and those who studied their development theorized their future. For example, in 1949, a writer for Popular Mechanics magazine looked at the most advanced computer available: It weighed 30 tons (27,216kg) and used 18,000 vacuum tubes. The unnamed writer predicted that, as vacuum tubes became more efficient, "Computers in the future may have only 1,000 vacuum tubes and perhaps weigh only 1½ tons [1,361kg]."[1]

By the late 1950s, computers were being used to aid scientists in a wide variety of fields, including the emerging sciences of manned spaceflight and satellite communications. The greatest breakthrough in early computer development came not through more efficient vacuum tubes but in advancements that *Popular Mechanics* calls "two of the most pivotal inventions in human history: the transistor, which came into widespread use in the mid-1950s, and the integrated circuit, or microchip, which intensified the march toward miniaturization a decade later."[2]

Integrated circuits—also called microchips—and interface cards can be seen in this interior view of the Apple II Plus, which was sold from 1978 to 1982.

Transistors stop, start, and control the flow of electricity through a circuit board with great precision and do so with greater efficiency than vacuum tubes. A modern computer chip can have millions of transistors to perform requested tasks. An integrated circuit, or microchip, enables transistors to work together with other electronic components such as capacitors and resistors. These advancements led to smaller and more powerful computers that were purchased by companies and universities across the United States and other countries. This, in turn, led to greater demand for computers and requests for time to use them. This resulted in the development of the mainframe computer.

Mainframes and Dumb Terminals

Mainframes served as centralized computers for companies and university departments. Complex cabling systems enabled multiple workers to utilize these mainframes from multiple locations within a building. Employees and students would sit at keyboards with monochrome screens that displayed information as green letters and numbers on a black screen. This keyboard-and-screen combination was known as a dumb terminal because, by itself, it was unable to perform any tasks; it served merely as a way of communicating with the mainframe. Each user had to log on in order to use the mainframe, but merely sitting at a dumb terminal and logging on did not guarantee access to the mainframe.

Mainframe technology was innovative but had limitations. Each mainframe had limited capacity for users and tasks. As requests from individuals and groups for access to the mainframes grew, computer owners began to schedule and restrict time on the mainframe. It became commonplace for computer users to sign up for overnight hours, when the mainframe was least requested. This concept of time-sharing was effective as long as the requests did not exceed the capacity of the system. Analysts began realizing that demand often exceeded mainframe capabilities in one location while computing power in another was under-utilized. By the late 1960s, developers began to study how mainframe resources and capacity could be shared across company locations or university buildings and campuses.

A significant advancement in connecting mainframes came when computer users convinced telephone companies to install special phone lines that were dedicated to handling data traffic only. In 1969, the U.S. Department of Defense's Advanced Research Projects Agency (ARPA) helped four universities in California and Utah connect their mainframes via dedicated phone lines to create the world's first computer network, called ARPANET. The first communication between computers of the ARPANET took place in October 1969, when an operator at the University of California, Los Angeles (UCLA) logged on to a computer at Stanford University at Palo Alto, California, approximately 400 miles (644km) away.

Evolving Communications

ARPANET was the beginning of a revolution in communications. A number of significant enhancements followed. Throughout the 1970s, developers created and refined computer communications. For example, in 1971, Ray Tomlinson, a programmer at the pioneering computer firm Bolt, Beranek, and Newman, developed the system for electronic mail, or e-mail. In 1974, Robert Kahn, an ARPANET program manager, and Vinton Cerf, an assistant professor at Stanford, developed the TCP/IP system of computer communications. TCP, or Transmission Control Protocol, is a system that facilitates the flow of digital data between computer networks. IP is short for Internet Protocol, which routes the data to its destination via a common address designation. TCP/IP remains the backbone of computer networks today.

By the 1980s, several computer networks existed in North America and Europe. Using an innovation called hypertext, individuals created documents, manuals, and databases with shortcuts called links, which enabled other users to access certain parts of files without having to move through the entire document. Hypertext links were particularly useful in tables of contents and indexes.

A British physicist named Tim Berners-Lee, working for the Swiss research center called CERN, saw that hypertext and links had a greater potential. He believed that they could enable users to access information from anywhere.

He called his idea of a vast network the World Wide Web. He believed:

> A person should be able to link with equal ease to any document wherever it happened to be stored . . . for the Web, the external link is what would allow it to actually become "worldwide." The important design element would be to ensure that when two groups had started to use the Web completely independently at different institutions, a person in one group could create a link to a document from the other with only a small incremental effort, and without having to merge the two document databases or even have access to the other system. If everyone on the Web could do this, then a single hypertext link could lead to an enormous, unbounded world.[3]

Access to this growing network was simplified by the development of browsers—computer programs that allowed users to view the hypertext on a screen and to use the links to jump through the documents as needed. Throughout the 1980s, more and more information was added to the World Wide Web as universities, institutions, and other developers made their databases available.

At first, access to the World Wide Web remained limited to those with access to mainframes and dumb terminals. However, at the same time, computer enthusiasts were striving to free themselves from the mainframe. Their achievement is commonly called the personal computer, or PC.

Enter the PC

The world's first PCs enabled users to create, edit, and save information on an individual basis without needing to be connected to a mainframe. The PC stored the data on an internal memory system called a hard drive, or on portable devices that contained thin ribbons of plastic coated with a magnetic material to facilitate data storage. The first of these storage devices for consumer use were 5.25-inch (133-mm) rectangles with a thin, flexible plastic outer shell; these came to be known as floppy disks. By the 1990s, that format was replaced by the 3.5-inch (89-mm) floppy disk, which was able to store more data in a smaller size.

The PC and the floppy disk enabled computer users to simplify many tasks in a work environment. For example, an individual using a PC could create a template of a standard type of correspondence such as a thank you letter, and then save it on a floppy disk. If another individual needed to send out a thank you letter, he or she simply borrowed the floppy disk and modified the template of the letter as appropriate. In the August 12, 1996, edition of *Business Week* magazine, Andy Reinhardt wrote there were "an estimated 5 billion [floppy disks] now in use"[4] worldwide, containing schedules, letters, invoices, contracts, school reports, job résumés, and much more.

In the mid-1980s 5.25-inch floppy disks were replaced by 3.5-inch disks, which were used widely through the late 1990s until they were made obsolete by CDs and DVDs.

As PCs became more affordable, they became a commonplace feature beyond the largest and wealthiest companies. Small to midsize businesses (SMBs) purchased them as well and installed business-related programs to perform a variety of tasks: Spreadsheet programs, such as Visicalc and Lotus 1-2-3, presented data in the form of tables and enabled companies to track inventory and simplify product ordering and billing through features that automated calculations; computer-assisted design programs, such as AutoCAD, and imaging software, such as Corel Draw and Adobe Photoshop, enabled users to create two-dimensional (and later three-dimensional) drawings without the need for specialized drafting tools.

Workplace Revolutions

The conjunction of the PC and specialized software changed how business was conducted. As late as the 1980s, businesses employed large numbers of individuals (often young women) in a secretarial pool or typing pool. Their sole job was to take recordings of memos, notes from meetings, and shorthand dictation, and generate typewritten company correspondence. These clerical positions disappeared as PCs and printers enabled individuals to generate their own memos and letters; fewer people were needed to perform the same tasks. Between 1989 and 2000, the number of individuals employed by the U.S. government in largely clerical jobs fell from more than 300,000 to 139,000. Similarly, where businesses had employed dozens of people to calculate, tabulate, and double-check numbers calculations, the introduction of spreadsheet software meant data-entry workers could enter and check their work automatically.

While the typing pool and the data-entry rooms fell silent, the rise of the PC led to the growth of the information technology (IT) division. Employees in this field installed and maintained computers, installed new software, and assisted users in their operations. They also helped businesses study and implement the connection of workplace PCs to the Internet. IT staff oversaw the implementation and expansion of e-mail, showing employees how they could collaborate with their colleagues without leaving their desks. Paper interoffice memos were replaced by e-mailed messages on a screen. IT professionals also helped develop and implement websites to promote their employers' operations, which vied for attention on the Web.

By the 1990s, IT professionals were updating the practice of networking PCs in different locations for improved functionality; hard drives with greater storage capacity and increased processing speeds were enabling teams of individuals to collaborate on documents and projects. PCs were connected through cables throughout buildings, creating a self-contained network that was accessible only to employees. Customer service employees working in the front office could communicate with back office staff such as supervisors or warehouse personnel. Orders or sales could

Becoming a Computer Application Software Engineer

Job Description: Computer application software engineers design, develop, install, and test software applications such as utility programs and general application software. In cloud computing settings, they may work with both internal/data center and external/cloud-based infrastructure. Some computer application software engineers design and produce commercially sold software suites; others design or customize applications for businesses or other organizations. An emerging field is cloud-based, cross-platform compatible game and application designs for cell phones, MP3 players, and other portable computers.

Education: Most entry-level computer application software engineer positions require a minimum of a bachelor's degree in computer science, software engineering, or related fields—although, for some positions, an associate's degree in software engineering or computer science is sufficient. Higher-level positions require additional education at the graduate level or on-the-job training.

Qualifications: Many positions require a degree plus experience in computer application software engineering. Proven knowledge of applications design and familiarity with cloud services environments, such as Amazon Web Services, Windows Azure, or Rackspace, are a plus. Proficiency in multiple programming languages such as Java, Ruby, or Python is particularly valuable.

Additional Information: Applications engineers must communicate with systems analysts, engineers, and programmers to obtain information on project limitations, performance requirements, and interfaces. They consult with clients in the design phase to determine client needs. After an application has been released, they help customers with maintenance issues. Excellent oral and written communication skills are very valuable.

Salary: $80,000 to more than $140,000 a year.

be instantly transmitted within a building or across a complex. For example, at the Portage Cache Store in Great Falls, Montana, when the webmaster in the back office received online orders, he would notify the front office sales staff to retrieve the ordered items; in turn, they would notify the sales manager, also in the back office, if stock needed to be replenished—all via an internal PC network.

The Portage Cache Store, with one location inside a U.S. Forest Service visitor center, had simple networking needs. However, larger businesses often found that their computing needs were no longer being served by individual PCs at workstations. Once again, IT professionals updated an earlier practice to meet these demands.

The Rise of the Server

By the end of the twentieth century, computing power and demand was growing exponentially every year. As computer programs became more complex and grew in size from kilobytes to megabytes, storage requirements grew as well. IT professionals recalled how centralized mainframes had once accommodated users from various locations and updated the idea with newer technology. They began installing servers in companies, schools, and government facilities to meet these demands. A server was similar to a mainframe in that it functioned as a centralized storage hub. But instead of being connected to dumb terminals,

An IT professional works in a large, contemporary data server filled with stacked servers.

these new server hubs were networked to fully functioning and independent PCs. A server was independent from—but accessible by—an organization's PCs. This innovation allowed individuals to store items such as music, image, or multimedia files, which might have overloaded one PC.

The first servers were often surplus computers with generic hard drives that were networked to other PCs via cables. Later servers were built to particular company specifications, with business-related hardware and software, and connected via telephone lines to remote locations. Servers handled dozens or hundreds of employee demands such as receiving and distributing e-mail and prioritizing requests for printing documents at a central printer.

One example of a networked server exists at the University of Maryland's Western Maryland Research and Education Center (WMREC). The 250-gigabyte server supplements the PCs used by the nearly two dozen employees in two buildings. It enables the staff to create backup copies of their important documents and to share important files without the need for e-mail. A user simply saves the document to a folder on the server's common hard drive to make it available to all with access to the server. The server also enables the storing of data and programming code related to several websites concerning the center's research and outreach programs—websites full of research information, helpful tips for landowners and farmers, and short videos on topics ranging from converting lawns to forests, to raising mushrooms for sale.

WMREC's modest server requirements were far overshadowed by the needs of the university's main campus in College Park, Maryland. There, thousands of students, faculty, and staff needed access to computing power for class schedules, assignments and exams, research and data analysis, and e-mail. They also needed high-speed Internet connections to access and develop websites with music and video features such as recordings of class lectures, video conferencing, and music or dance performances. Similar demands encountered by other organizations worldwide led to the development of the data center.

The Data Center

The modern data center is far more than a server or two in a spare room inside an organization's building. Instead, the data center is contained within its own building, purposely built to house computing power and the people who run it. Racks of networked servers fill the floor. Centralized terminals enable IT staff to oversee operations. Data from PCs throughout the organization flows in and out through dedicated fiber-optic data lines.

These independent structures also have specific needs to maintain the efficiency of the server operations and the security of the data. In order for the servers to work properly, they need to be kept within specific temperature and humidity ranges; data centers have their own separate heating and air-conditioning systems to maintain optimum conditions. The centers also need backup generators to ensure continued service if electrical power is interrupted, and specialized systems to connect the generators to the data center's power grid. These systems are expensive. According to IBM's vice president of site and facilities management Steve Sams, "About 60% of the costs [of a data center] are the electrical and mechanical costs. That's the air conditioners, the storage tanks for generators, the UPSes (uninterruptible power supplies)."[5] Sams noted that IBM's data centers "represent about 6% of our floor space and 35% of our total energy consumption."[6]

Data centers also require security systems for the personnel who run them. Video camera surveillance and onsite security guards protect both the interior and exterior. Access is restricted to authorized individuals who have passed background security checks and who possess specialized training. They enter the data center itself and individual areas via specialized access cards or key codes, or via biometric systems, which identify staff by physical characteristics, such as through fingerprint identification.

Creating and maintaining a data center, therefore, involves a considerable financial investment. Organizations need to examine both the positive and the negative aspects of such an investment.

Economic Benefits and Drawbacks

Data centers have a wide variety of benefits for organizations wishing to consolidate their computing resources. The servers in a data center provide a single source for the storage and processing of employee records, customer orders, research data and results, e-mail, and more. They also provide a central location for backups from an organization's PCs or networks. Additionally, they enable organizations to concentrate the majority of their IT personnel in a central location.

Data centers, however, also have a wide variety of economic drawbacks. The personnel need to continually update their specialized training, so that they can keep up with the latest versions of server software and hardware. They also must install new and upgraded programs, as well as troubleshoot and fix computer malfunctions. The data can be threatened if the exterior is hit by an earthquake or a hurricane, or if the interior suffers from fire or vandalism. The data may also be at risk simply by the age of the building. IBM's Sams says that while many data centers are designed to last fifteen to twenty years, "no one has a crystal ball"[7] that can predict if a center built today will last that long. A study in 2010 by the Canadian government's auditor general found that many of its data centers were "supported by old infrastructure and are at risk of breaking down. A breakdown would have wide and severe consequences—at worst, the government could no longer conduct its business and deliver services to Canadians."[8]

One of the most challenging aspects of proposing, developing, and maintaining a data center is the cost. Prices of construction materials, computer hardware and software, and electric rates may rise before the project is completed. New technologies in security, such as advanced biometrics, may need to be installed after construction is completed.

Above all, the capacity of the servers may be reached in a shorter time than expected.

These factors have contributed to a new movement in data storage. Organizations worldwide are deciding that the costs of maintaining their current data centers, as well as the prospects of paying for new ones, are impractical. They believe that cloud computing is the future of data management.

The Emergence of "The Cloud"

In the early days of the Internet, IT professionals often drew diagrams that described how computers were connected to each other, using cloud-shaped bubbles in between the two to symbolize the vast network of telecommunications hardware and software. Later users adopted the cloud symbol to designate storage facilities that were not on a PC's local, or internal, hard drive. In this way, servers and the data centers that followed were early forms of clouds.

Businesses and organizations took advantage of these early cloud designs to build virtual private networks (VPNs). These allowed authorized users to access their information via the Internet regardless of where they happened to be. While their data might have been accessible on their work PC or on the server, it was considered "in the cloud" because it stayed on the hard drive where it was stored. They did not need to download large or sensitive files onto a computer at a hotel or a library in order to work with them. They could work from home or from anywhere they could access the World Wide Web. The data remained secure behind Internet-based passwords and authentication processes.

For many casual computer users, however, their first encounter with the cloud came through their e-mail system. In many early e-mail programs, users downloaded every message for storage on their PC's hard drive. By the late 1990s, however, services such as Yahoo! Mail and Google's Gmail allowed users to view, print, forward, and reply to their messages without having to download them. The messages remained on the provider's server until they were

WHY IS IT CALLED THE CLOUD?

The Internet is a network of networks. Millions of computers and devices all over the world are in networks that are connected to other networks in a complex web made up of principal data routes, core routers, exchange points, service providers, servers, fiber-optic cables, satellites, telephone lines, and WiFi. A graphic representation of the inteterconnections in one part of the Internet looks like this:

An image of a cloud is used in computer diagrams as shorthand for the Internet's complex infrastructure. The cloud has become the metaphor for the Internet and the services delivered through it.

Source: Internet map by the Opte Project. "Internet Map." *English Wikipedia*. April 28, 2013.

"Two-Pizza Teams"

In 2001, Jeff Bezos, the founder of Amazon.com, was trying to determine the best use for its data centers' excess computing capacity. He enlisted small groups of five to eight employees to come up with ideas, no matter how unusual. According to Robert D. Hof, writing in *Bloomberg Businessweek* magazine, "these 'two-pizza teams,' [as] Bezos calls them because each team can be fed with two large pies, have become Amazon's prime innovation engines."

Bezos's "two-pizza teams" were designed to work independently in order to innovate and test their visions without outside influence. One of the ideas that came from a two-pizza team was the notion of making the excess computing capacity available to the public. When this new concept, called Amazon Web Services, debuted in 2002, it revolutionized personal and business computing in the cloud.

Robert D. Hof. "Jeff Bezos' Risky Bet." *Bloomberg Businessweek,* November 12, 2006. www.businessweek.com/stories/2006-11-12/jeff-bezos-risky-bet.

deleted by the reader. These services operate in the cloud; the hard drive of the user's PC contains none of the messages unless the user specifically downloads them. Another common use of the cloud includes Internet banking, in which users can access their account information and pay bills without needing to install specialized software on a PC.

The use of the cloud became more widespread in the early twenty-first century due, in part, to the efforts of Amazon, the company that had revolutionized book sales on the World Wide Web. Ideas from small teams of Amazon employees grew into a branch of the business called Amazon Web Services (AWS). The ideas helped to revolutionize the computing industry.

Amazon's Innovation

The concept behind AWS was making the excess storage capacity at Amazon data centers available to customers. Today, AWS is a division within Amazon that encompasses a variety of cloud-based services that helped to bring the cloud and cloud computing to individuals and businesses around the world. Instead of purchasing servers, customers can sign up with Amazon to rent server storage capacity through a service now called Simple Storage Service, or S3. Another service, Elastic Compute Cloud, or EC2, enables customers to purchase computer processing power to host websites. The concept of AWS was amazingly successful among computer technologists; when EC2 was quietly launched in a test mode in

2006, all of the available test slots were reserved in less than five hours.

Within a decade, both S3 and EC2 were being used by hundreds of companies. For example, in 2012 a new company called Cue filtered documents, Facebook updates, calendar appointments, and more to create reminders sent to a user's computer or smartphone. Daniel Gross, Cue's cofounder, says that he would need six times as many engineers to operate and maintain enough servers to meet his customers' demands.

Other technology companies took notice of Amazon's services. In 2008, computing giants Google and Microsoft entered the cloud computing business. Neha Prakash, writing for the digital innovation website Mashable.com, shared that:

> The Google App Engine brought low-cost computing and storage services, popularizing the concept; by 2009, Google Apps allowed people to store documents within the cloud. Microsoft followed suit with Windows Azure, solidifying the cloud as a market that the tech giants would be expanding and competing in.[9]

Apple also waded into cloud computing when they announced the iCloud service in 2011. It enables users to synchronize their photos, music, documents, and more across a variety of Apple devices by way of the company's cloud servers. That same year, Amazon unveiled Cloud Drive, offering five gigabytes of free storage through S3 for its everyday customers, allowing them to store and replay their music via the Amazon Cloud Player.

Regardless of the company behind it, cloud computing services share a common model. The model demonstrates the belief that computing power should be as accessible as any other everyday utility.

The Cloud Computing Model

The appeal of these cloud computing services lies in the utility model. In the same way that water, electric, and gas companies charge customers only for what they use, Amazon,

Google, Microsoft, and others charge the customer only for the storage space used, or the computing power used.

These aspects of cloud computing are particularly appealing to individuals involved in young Internet companies, called startups. One of the hottest startups of 2012 was Pinterest, a social network that allows users to share interesting photos on personal pin boards for friends to see. In March 2012, *Fortune* magazine noted that Pinterest was "the fastest-growing website of all time,"[10] registering a 52 percent jump in one month. In November 2011, Pinterest had 5 million unique visitors each month; four months later that number skyrocketed to nearly 18 million.

In the past, such explosive growth would have forced Pinterest into making significantly large capital expenditures for more servers and more personnel, and, in the meantime, site users might have experienced slow service or lost data as Pinterest's current servers tried to meet the growing demand. Additionally, if customer interest fell after the new servers had been ordered and delivered, the company would have been saddled with the burden of their costs and their unused capacity. Pinterest's developers, however, chose to work in the cloud from the beginning. Using Amazon's cloud computing services, the company was able to meet the increased demand that came with increased popularity. All it took was online requests to Amazon for more server space. In a June 4, 2012, interview, Pinterest's technical operations and infrastructure lead Ryan Park said the company had 8 billion items, consisting of 410 terabytes of data, on Amazon's S3 servers. He noted, "It would have been very hard for us to [grow] as quickly [as we did] without AWS."[11]

In the same way that a household's electric or gas bill rises and falls month to month based on how much a furnace or an air conditioner runs, the price of cloud computing services rises and falls based on how much server space a company needs or how much computing power it uses. Yet those who use cloud computing believe it is money well spent. Cue's Gross estimates that AWS costs his company approximately $100,000 a month but that it would cost "probably $2 million to do it ourselves." He

Pinterest, a photo-sharing website and app that allows users to create and manage theme-based image collections, met growing client demand by using Amazon's cloud computing services.

noted that cloud computing means that he does not need to worry about server-related capital expenditure, admitting that "I don't even know what the ballpark [cost] for a server is—for me, it would be like knowing what the price of a sword is."[12]

Advocates of the cloud computing model, such as Cue's Gross or Pinterest's Park, tout its flexibility, accessibility, and apparent simplicity. Data is stored offsite on a remote server. Server space is scalable, meaning that it can be both added and subtracted as needed. An Internet connection is all that is required to access the data and to manage storage capacity. Yet, there is an amazing amount of technology that goes into cloud computing. At the heart of this is a three-layered suite of customizable services that computer programmers call "the stack."

CHAPTER 2

"The Stack": SaaS, IaaS, and PaaS

Technology is an essential part of everyday life in the twenty-first century. It is not necessary to fully understand how a computer or a cell phone works in order to use either one. It is, however, necessary to understand how each device will be used in order to use it efficiently. For example, a computer comes in myriad designs and has virtually limitless options for personal customization. Some individuals use a computer to surf the World Wide Web, to read and send e-mail, or to complete school or work assignments; for them, a basic model is usually sufficient. Other individuals use a computer to design or play games, to create music, or to run a business; for them, a computer needs to have additional memory, or enhanced graphics capabilities, or specialized programs. They require a computer that is fully customized to suit their needs.

In the same way, cloud computing can be tailored to meet the requirements of computer users, program developers, and business owners. At the heart of cloud computing is "the stack." It contains three layers of customizable services that can be employed to meet the user's demands.

Each layer of "the stack" has an acronym that ends with "aaS," which is short for "as-a-Service." The "aaS" concept grew as companies began changing programs from traditional software (that was purchased or downloaded) to software that performed completely through the Web. One of the earliest examples of this shift in computing was online e-mail.

E-Mail in the Cloud

It is important to understand that the technology of e-mail has progressed significantly since the 1990s. Early messages were text-only, and users downloaded each message onto their PC's hard drive. As the volume of messages grew, and as users found ways to add graphics, photographs, music, and video to them, they discovered that the limits of their hard drives were being challenged.

By the start of the twenty-first century, however, new types of e-mail programs, which came to be known as web mail, began to gain popularity. Companies such as Google and Yahoo provided services that performed all the traditional tasks of electronic messaging, but with two significant differences: The user did not need to install or maintain software and did not have to worry about storage space on their personal devices. Web mail programs offer virtually limitless storage capacity for each account. In fact, when subscribers to Google's Gmail visit the service's homepage to log in, they find a counter that shows how much storage space is available on Google's servers. The counter is continually counting up.

This concept of Internet-based software intrigued a group of developers in California. In 1999, they created Salesforce and launched their first program, Salesforce.com, from a small apartment in San Francisco. Their intent was to create and market accounting and business development programs that were fully accessible through the Internet. It was a revolutionary concept.

Salesforce Takes Off

Salesforce was entering the field of customer relationship management (CRM), which enables companies to organize and automate sales, marketing, customer service, and technical support. In a 2002 interview with *InfoWorld* magazine,

Dave Moellenhoff, Salesforce's co-founder and chief technical officer, said:

> Up until we came along there was high-end CRM [software that] was too expensive. Most people in the small-to-[midsize] market couldn't afford a $5,000-[per-employee] license. We were trying to take this functionality that was reserved for the very few privileged with money and bring it to everybody else because everyone could use it.[13]

Salesforce's innovations meant that SMB owners who subscribed to their service did not have to worry about installing the program, keeping it updated, or buying new versions. It was all online, and Salesforce took care of implementing all updates. In addition, the business owner did not need to hire specialized trainers to instruct employees in its use. Salesforce had a simple interface that enabled users to learn as they worked. The service enabled businesses to pay bills, manage sales contacts, create reports, and more. The Salesforce model turned out to be extremely appealing. Within a year of its 1999 launch, the company had fifteen hundred customers with thirty thousand employees subscribed to its service. A year later, there were thirty-five hundred customers with fifty-three thousand subscribers, and by the time *InfoWorld* interviewed Moellenhoff, Salesforce had fifty-seven hundred customers with seventy-six thousand subscribers. *InfoWorld*'s Brian Fonseca wrote that Moellenhoff "sees the future in software—particularly CRM solutions—as a service."[14]

Moellenhoff was echoing a phrase introduced a year earlier by the Software & Information Industry Association (SIIA). In February 2001, the association developed a publication that introduced a new phrase and a new acronym to the growing world of computing. The acronym was SaaS.

SaaS

In the world of business, companies or associations often create specialized publications to introduce or serve as a guide to a particular issue or product. The SIIA document, *Software as a Service: Strategic Backgrounder,* provided important information about the rising tide of online software. In addition, the authors coined the phrase "Software-as-a-Service" and its acronym "SaaS" (pronounced "sass"). In an attempt to reduce confusion over a variety of competing and confusing acronyms currently in use, they instead suggested this one shorthand phrase to encompass them all:

Software as a Service (SaaS) . . . is heralded by many as the new wave in application software distribution. . . . [T]o avoid confusion SIIA refers to the model generally as software as a service.

In the software as a service model, the application, or service, is deployed from a centralized data center

Virtualization

One of the revolutions that make cloud computing possible is called virtualization. Virtualization separates the operating system (OS) from the underlying hardware. It enables servers in data centers to store more information than ever before, making it possible for a single server to be available for numerous uses.

The key to virtualization is a device called a hypervisor, which is a set of hardware and software connected directly to a computer's storage disks. The OS is then installed on the hypervisor. With hypervisors installed on a data center's servers, operators can move an OS from one server to another as easily as a PC user can move a file from one folder to another. Virtualization also enables multiple copies of different operating systems, called instances, to be installed on a particular hypervisor. This allows servers to accommodate applications that run on Windows, Linux, and more, as long as the OS instance is installed on the hypervisor.

A virtualized server is a lot like an apartment building. In an apartment building, each apartment has its own lights, water, and plumbing to accommodate its residents; in virtualization, each OS instance has its own applications to accommodate its user.

across a network . . . providing access and use on a recurring fee basis. Users "rent," "subscribe to," "are assigned," or "are granted access to" the applications from a central provider. . . . The core value of software as a service is providing access to, and management of, a commercially available application. The potential benefits of the model are significant for both the vendor and the customer.[15]

SIIA's designation and acronym caught on. SaaS became part of the cloud computing vocabulary and slowly began to attract advocates from around the world. One of them is a New Zealand businessman named Ben Kepes.

"SaaS Changes All This"

Ben Kepes is a cloud computing analyst for Diversity Limited, a business strategy consultancy. He explains that SaaS helps businesses avoid both emergency and routine chores. He remembered a business trip during which he left his laptop in the back of a taxi:

> It was a disaster. Sensitive documents, customer data, all gone. It's a real headache for IT trying to restore everything from a backup—that's if a backup even existed. Even if you didn't lose your laptop, IT had its hands full with patches, updates, installs, and all the server and software maintenance. SaaS changes all this. Instead of IT, or even the business owner having to manage e-mail, accounting software, file storage, collaboration, customer relationship management data, these applications are provided as a service from a vendor who's responsible for all the hard stuff.[16]

Other business owners agreed with Kepes that SaaS held numerous advantages for their commercial interests. As the twenty-first century progressed, other companies began to follow in the footsteps of Salesforce.com by offering their own SaaS-based CRM solutions, and businesses large and small around the world adopted SaaS for their CRM needs. For example, in 2012, the computer giant Hewlett-Packard began moving its worldwide CRM to SaaS pioneer Salesforce.com. That same year, a free neighborhood newspaper in London, England, the *Hackney Citizen*, moved its CRM to SaaS through online-services company Lineup. Keith Magnum, the newspaper's managing director, believed that implementing SaaS would "help support and enhance our continuing advertising business growth."[17]

No matter which SaaS provider a business chooses for its CRM, its core features help businesses keep current and recruit new advertisers, track invoices, fulfill orders, and manage customer complaints and comments. However, with sensitive data, such as financial, personnel, and health care details, there was initial hesitation about inputting such information into the cloud for fear that it would not be secure. Implementing SaaS for these business matters posed other challenges for SaaS providers.

From the Front Office to the Back Office

Many of the world's business owners who had eagerly adopted SaaS solutions for e-mail, customer order data, or newsletter generation were less enthusiastic about using cloud computing for more sensitive information. While they were comfortable putting front office data in the cloud, they were less so in placing back office data there. They were concerned about the security of placing pension records, employment histories, and worker identification information, such as U.S. Social Security numbers, in the cloud rather than on a local server.

SaaS providers worked to ensure that customer data was encrypted and secure. The success of cloud-based backup SaaS companies, such as Carbonite, showed that sensitive information in the cloud could be both accessible and protected. At the same time, a new generation of human resources (HR) managers who used SaaS-based programs in their personal lives enthusiastically embraced Web 2.0 in general and cloud computing specifically. HR departments are responsible for employee records, such as names and addresses, job histories, identification records, performance reviews, and much more, in a field called human capital management (HCM). SaaS developers worked to meet HCM's specialized cloud computing needs for accessibility and security.

One successful developer of SaaS-based HCM services is Workday, based in Pleasanton, California. The company was founded in 2005 to meet a variety of business financial needs, including the specialized needs of HCM. Since then, the company has become a world leader in providing SaaS-based solutions for hundreds of clients. They serve businesses as diverse as fruit grower Chiquita Brands International and automotive manufacturer Toyota. They also serve a variety of education institutions across the United States, with Brown University in Providence, Rhode Island, signing on as one of their new clients in 2012.

Brown University chose Workday to update its antiquated and overloaded HCM services. The university's previous system had been based on a server installed in 1991. According to Roberta Gordon, the project director for Human Capital Management and Finance System Replacement at Brown, "Probably fewer than 50 people [out of Brown's approximately 11,000 employees] had access to it, and those were the people who entered the data into the system. Nowadays people are used to doing things on their own—online banking, online purchasing, online everything. And our HR system didn't have that." In 2012, Brown's HCM made the transition to Workday. Gordon says Workday means that "Brown employees can go in and view their benefits, their time off, their mailing addresses, their emergency contacts right from a single place."[18]

The new system frees Brown's HR and IT departments from needing to maintain, patch, upgrade, or repair their local server-based software. SaaS providers perform these necessary chores as part of the company's service. For example, Workday issues patches and upgrades three times a year. Its April 2013 update included expanded compatibility with smartphones and tablets, including for the first time, those devices using Google's Android operating system. The success of back office SaaS applications from Workday and others demonstrates that more and more businesses and organizations are willing to place their trust in cloud-based systems. This trust is also beginning to expand into the personal computing environment.

SaaS for Artistic Development

The traditional personal computing model meant individuals selected a particular operating system, such as from Microsoft or from Apple, and then selected which programs best suited their needs. Sometimes the model was reversed; users needed to learn a particular program, but it was only available for use on one particular system. SaaS avoids both models because these programs are platform-independent, meaning that they can run on any system, as long as the computer is connected to the Internet.

SaaS-based programs enable the user to create a wide range of digital media. For example, Google's suite of programs called Google Docs allows users to create documents, spreadsheets, and websites in a variety of file formats; they are automatically saved to the user's cloud-based account, which makes them accessible using any Internet connection. British lecturer and futurist Christopher Barnatt used it to write his book *A Brief Guide to Cloud Computing,* sharing screenshots of his book's drafts and folders as illustrations. Adobe's Creative Cloud suite enables subscribers who use its popular artistic software, such as Photoshop for image editing and InDesign for designing publications, to store and access their creations in the cloud across a variety of devices, and to collaborate with team members on projects from a single company dashboard. Individual users can also take advantage of the Creative Cloud suite by subscribing to individual programs as needed.

This pay-as-you-go model is widespread throughout cloud computing. The success and expansion of SaaS shows that even novice computer users can work in the cloud. Yet, SaaS is only one layer of the cloud computing stack. For computer developers who are intent on creating their own programs within the cloud, Infrastructure-as-a-Service (IaaS) is the way to go.

IaaS

IaaS (pronounced "eye-as") was the second layer of cloud computing to be developed. "Infrastructure" means the underlying foundation or basic framework of a system or an organization; in the world of computers, it often applies to the machine's operating system. Consequently, IaaS refers to the foundation of the cloud-based server upon which a computer developer can construct a system to meet a particular need.

This layer of "the stack" goes to the heart of computing services. In the same way that SaaS provides an alternative to a business or an organization purchasing a program or suite of programs, IaaS provides an alternative to creating a data center. Instead of calculating capital expenditure costs for servers, security, and the physical structure of a data center, businesses or organizations can opt for IaaS-based cloud services. Cloud computing analyst Ben Kepes points out one of the risks of building a data center:

> Under a traditional model, a CIO [chief information-officer] or CTO [chief technical officer] would need to plot and estimate load demand [and] peak demand, and build infrastructure that met those potential demands. And of course, given that it's on-premise infrastructure, they'd have to do that months, even years before the event, so they'd have to try to intuit what their load would be twelve months down the track, get approval for capital funding for that infrastructure, and have it sitting there. Now of course if that CIO or CTO was completely wrong in that capacity planning exercise, that infrastructure would go to waste, and then all that capital investment would go to waste.[19]

The key to creating a data center that would meet current and future needs would be to have server infrastructure adequate to meet anticipated peak demands. The pitfalls there are twofold: In the first case, the estimates are too optimistic, and anticipated traffic never materializes, so the server infrastructure is underused, proving the capital expenditure to be more than necessary; in the second case, the estimates are too pessimistic, and demand far outstrips capacity, so the servers cannot handle the load, leading to system outages and failures, proving the capital expenditure was less than necessary. IaaS seeks to help businesses avoid these pitfalls by making server computing customizable for each customer.

"Making Infrastructure Self-Service"

One of the first advantages to IaaS is that it helps businesses manage expenses. Each business owner faces two types of expenses. Everyday expenses can be predicted and controlled with a budget. Each is called an operating expense (OpEx). Such expenses include building rent, electricity, and personnel wages. One-time expenses, such as the purchase of a building or a vehicle, have an initial and large expense, which is considered to be capital expenditure, or CapEx, and then smaller recurring payments over time, which is OpEx. In the traditional computing environment, installing and maintaining servers involved both CapEx and OpEx. With cloud computing, however, choosing IaaS enables businesses to eliminate the initial CapEx because the servers are owned by the provider. Server costs are, therefore, reduced to the recurring OpEx rental rates.

IaaS, however, has a greater appeal for many customers. Erik Carlin is a senior architect for cloud with Rackspace, a cloud services provider. He believes that IaaS "in its most fundamental form is about making infrastructure self-service."[20] Self-service is a widespread concept in the retail environment. An individual can perform self-service banking to get cash through an ATM and then use a grocery store self-service checkout lane to purchase items for dinner. In these self-service environments, the bank owns and maintains the ATM, and the grocery store owns and maintains the scanner. In the IaaS cloud environment, the provider owns and maintains the infrastructure equipment. The customer then chooses how best to use it.

The self-service idea also pertains to what items the IaaS customer chooses. At the ATM, the customer chooses the best options for cash by withdrawing $20, $40, or more. At the grocery store, he or she can decide on the best options for pizza for dinner by buying the individual ingredients for the crust and the toppings, or by buying a frozen one that only requires baking. With IaaS, the customer chooses the best options for the business by configuring and operating the software, database, and system that is built upon the infrastructure. In the same way that a grocery store offers many different ways to make a pizza, IaaS provides a menu of options from which to choose. It is up to each customer to choose which ingredients of IaaS are most important for his or her business.

Compute and Storage

There are five different ingredients of IaaS: Compute, Storage, Network, Database, and Monitoring and Autoscale.

Cloud Bursting

When businesses or organizations wish to create additional data center capacity for a short and defined period of time, they can engage in a technique called "cloud bursting." Cloud bursting is an example of a hybrid cloud model, in which a customer has a mixture of in-house data centers and virtual server space. In this model, the customer rents additional virtual server capacity for peak demand and then returns to an average nonpeak-demand capacity. It is similar to organizations, such as parks and recreation departments, that have a set number of individuals working for them year-round, but then, during busy months, hire additional staff such as lifeguards, groundskeepers, and so on.

One example of cloud bursting occurs when TV network ABC broadcasts *Dancing with the Stars*. The network recognizes that this show is very popular and that there will be a surge of interest on their website when it comes time to vote for the contestants. To meet this demand, the company bursts into a hybrid cloud to accommodate the increased traffic; when the voting ends, they return to their year-round capacity. This allows them to avoid spending for additional server capacity that will be idle for most of the year.

Each ingredient, or module, represents an IaaS feature that businesses can choose to deploy to serve their needs. Compute is the most fundamental part of IaaS; it represents the ability to transfer data from physical servers in a data center to cloud-based virtualized server instances. Additionally, Compute enables users to select which type of operating system they wish to run on the virtual servers, such as Windows, Macintosh, or Linux, and how much disk space and memory capacity they wish to have for each virtual server.

The second module to consider is Storage. This is separate from the storage in Compute in the same way that a PC has both memory for the operating system and memory for user files. With Storage, each IaaS user must determine what type of data will be stored, and how often it will be accessed. Block-level storage is similar to connecting an external hard drive to a PC, but in IaaS, the hard drive is virtual and is created within a server. The block then serves as a separate storage facility and can then be used for storing databases or important files. An alternative method is called file-level storage, which is often useful for storing raw files such as photos, videos, and music files, or for placing backup copies of files. File-level storage tends to be simpler to use than block-level, but may result in particular files being placed onto separate virtual servers in different data centers. This may lead to difficulty in accessing user data.

One of the ways that IaaS providers reduce these roadblocks is through content delivery networks (CDNs), which work to make user information as available as possible. Even in an age of broadband Internet access, information takes time to cross countries or continents from a cloud provider to a user. A CDN helps overcome what Kepes calls the "tyranny of distance"[21] of the Internet.

> To illustrate the value of a CDN, take, for example, the case of an ecommerce website hosted in the United States with most website visitors also located in the United States. The time that it takes the product catalogue images to load is probably quite fast, since the server and those accessing it are both located in the same general geography. What would happen, however, if the products suddenly became popular in China, or South Africa? The time to download the product images from the US-based server would increase for these global visitors. CDNs solve this problem by taking image files and putting them on servers all over the world. Then, when a request [for those images] comes in, the CDN serves it from the location closest to the requestor. The webmaster need only upload the image to one place, their server, and the CDN takes care of the rest, distributing the file all over the world for optimal performance. By utilizing a CDN, Cloud vendors solve some of the issues created by a move to centralized infrastructure.[22]

A CDN is, however, only as efficient as the provider's system of moving data. That is where the module called Network comes into play.

Network, Database, and Monitoring and Autoscale

IaaS providers work to ensure that user data moves quickly and efficiently. In a traditional onsite data center, the IT department had to ensure that the various computers and servers communicated through the efficient switching and routing of data, and had to ensure a consistent connection to the Internet. The Network module takes care of all that. It also employs load balancing, which is particularly helpful for rapidly growing websites by ensuring that no one virtual server is overloaded by the increased traffic.

As this traffic increases, the website's administrators can deploy the Database module, which will enable them to analyze their site's data. They may also choose to employ Monitoring and Autoscale. The Monitoring portion enables them to track their peak usage and any potential outages, and Autoscale enables them to add virtual servers automatically to meet peak demand. For example, Pinterest's Ryan Park comments that Autoscale enables his company to reduce the number of servers they run under IaaS during overnight hours when traffic to the site is reduced.

IaaS originated with two services offered by Amazon: Elastic Compute Cloud (EC2) and Simple Storage Service (S3). Today, dozens of companies around the world, including computing giants Google and Microsoft, offer IaaS solutions for businesses and organizations. Part of the marketing appeal of IaaS is that businesses can use it to enter cloud computing in several ways.

IaaS Delivery Models

Once a business or organization has made the decision to move from its in-house data center infrastructure and has decided which IaaS modules to use, another decision remains before data can be migrated to a cloud provider. The

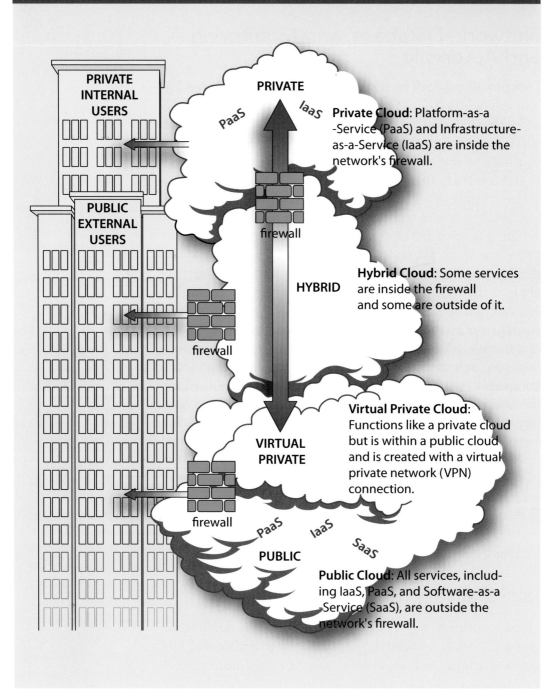

PRIVATE INTERNAL USERS

PUBLIC EXTERNAL USERS

PRIVATE

PaaS   IaaS

firewall

HYBRID

firewall

VIRTUAL PRIVATE

firewall

PaaS   IaaS   SaaS

PUBLIC

Private Cloud: Platform-as-a-Service (PaaS) and Infrastructure-as-a-Service (IaaS) are inside the network's firewall.

Hybrid Cloud: Some services are inside the firewall and some are outside of it.

Virtual Private Cloud: Functions like a private cloud but is within a public cloud and is created with a virtual private network (VPN) connection.

Public Cloud: All services, including IaaS, PaaS, and Software-as-a-Service (SaaS), are outside the network's firewall.

user needs to decide which type of cloud he or she wishes to develop. The choice made often depends on budget, ease of use, and security concerns. The choices are public cloud, private cloud, or hybrid cloud.

Public cloud is the least expensive and easiest to use. In this type, the user chooses to deploy one or more modules within an account with a cloud provider, and the user's data becomes stored on the provider's virtual servers. The expenses are lower than an in-house data center because the organization is just one of many using the provider's service; costs are spread out among the clients. Several types of organizations can benefit from using a public cloud. For example, a startup with no server infrastructure can start from scratch with one. An SMB that anticipates adding features to its Internet presence, which will bring increased traffic to its site, may also benefit from a public cloud. An established company that is taking on a project that will require significantly larger staff or data center infrastructure can rent public cloud space for the duration of the project. Developers and organizations can choose to build their public cloud through providers such as Amazon, Rackspace, or HP Cloud.

Private cloud, on the other hand, is more expensive and more labor-intensive than a public cloud. In this design, a company rents from a provider one or more specific servers that are dedicated solely to the particular customer. Consequently, this is the most secure type of cloud. Providers of private cloud services include CloudStack, Eucalyptus, and OpenNebula.

In between these two types is the hybrid cloud, in which an organization rents physical server space, or uses its own infrastructure, and rents virtual servers on demand on an as-needed basis. Christopher Barnatt says, "As a common example, a company may choose to run all of its applications on dedicated physical servers [from a cloud provider], but to store its data on virtual server instances. Or a business may rent virtual server instances by the hour to cope with occasional peak processing demands or to service occasional high levels of web traffic."[23] The common feature among these models is that each has the flexibility and scalability that are hallmarks of cloud computing.

Vendor Lock-In

Many corporations considering moving to the cloud are reluctant to do so because of the possibility of vendor lock-in. In a cloud computing environment, vendors provide a user-friendly way to move data to their servers, but customers may discover that it is less easy to move data out to another cloud. The data has been stored using the provider's proprietary methods, meaning that it has been stored in a way that it is only readable in their cloud environment, leaving the customer locked in to that provider.

Internet solutions group director Bill Gerhardt of computing giant Cisco Systems notes, "Customers ask: 'If I give you all this data, how do I retrieve that data if I want to go somewhere else?' Many cloud companies don't have a clear exit route."

Many cloud providers are working to reduce the possibility of lock-in by ensuring that their programming language is open source, which means that it is nonproprietary and can be deployed in any operating situation. An open-source language called OpenStack was developed by Rackspace and NASA, and, in less than two years since its debut, it has been adopted by companies around the world, from PayPal to Australia's University of Melbourne.

For companies that want more than SaaS, but feel that they are not ready to move completely to the cloud through IaaS, a third layer of the cloud computing stack is an option. This option is called Platform-as-a-Service, or PaaS.

PaaS

In the world of cloud computing, PaaS exists at the middle of the cloud computing stack between IaaS at the base and SaaS at the top. In the same way that artists consider the color orange more than yellow but not quite red, computer technologists consider PaaS (pronounced "pass") as being more than IaaS but not quite SaaS. With PaaS, the basic ingredients of the IaaS modules are preselected by the provider. Kepes likens the difference between PaaS and IaaS to a collection of ingredients needed to bake a cake. IaaS consists of modules that exist individually, such as "cocoa, eggs, butter, flour, and sugar," which the customer has to choose and blend in the correct proportions to create the cake. PaaS, on the other hand, is "a cake box mix where you just add eggs"[24] because the majority of the ingredients are already in place. With PaaS, the customer does not need to choose and deploy the IaaS modules individually. The customer simply chooses how to build on top of those modules.

One of the advantages of PaaS is that it provides a common environment upon which a single developer or a team of developers can build. Customers can choose a PaaS with an operating system or a programming language with which their programmers and app developers are already familiar. This enables them to build and deploy their creations without worrying if the programming will work in the cloud environment's operating system. Businesses can also import, or push, established applications to the cloud's PaaS with no loss of functionality, as long as the applications and the PaaS framework have a common coding language. In the words of a 2012 report from cloud provider ActiveState Software, Inc., PaaS is "essential to cloud-computing efficiency: Without a PaaS, each application would have to be customized to run on each type (and in some cases, each instance) of infrastructure . . . [making it] an expensive and impractical option."[25] Consequently, the right PaaS makes migrating to the cloud fairly straightforward and often means a significant savings in time and expense.

All PaaS layers provide users with a standardized framework of security, signup, and log-in functions by imposing a single model for managing authorization and authentication for any SaaS application running on top of it. But not all PaaS layers are the same, and, therefore, have varying capabilities, based on their origins.

HOW THE DIFFERENT SERVICE MODELS IN THE CLOUD "STACK UP"

The customer and the provider are responsible for different components of the stack in each of the service delivery models. In the traditional model, the customer controls all aspects, while in the Software-as-a-Service (SaaS) model, the service provider has the most control.

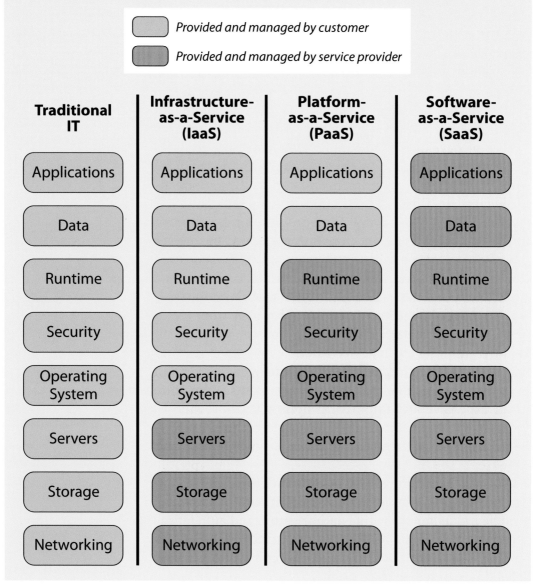

Provided and managed by customer

Provided and managed by service provider

Traditional IT	Infrastructure-as-a-Service (IaaS)	Platform-as-a-Service (PaaS)	Software-as-a-Service (SaaS)
Applications	Applications	Applications	Applications
Data	Data	Data	Data
Runtime	Runtime	Runtime	Runtime
Security	Security	Security	Security
Operating System	Operating System	Operating System	Operating System
Servers	Servers	Servers	Servers
Storage	Storage	Storage	Storage
Networking	Networking	Networking	Networking

PaaS Capabilities

Cloud providers have developed a variety of PaaS layers to serve different functions and to have different capabilities. In general, there are three types of PaaS layers. One type is tied to a particular operating environment, such as Amazon Web Services (AWS) or the Microsoft Azure cloud. Others are open source, enabling developers to create, test, and run their applications in a variety of multiple programming languages. A third type enables developers to integrate with an established SaaS environment. Salesforce, a pioneer in SaaS, created one of the first offerings of PaaS called Force.com in 2007. This PaaS provides a framework upon which Salesforce's customers can build. For example, an Australian applications development company called Trineo built customized PaaS applications for a firm called Menumate. Menumate uses Salesforce's SaaS CRM to serve the hotel and hospitality industry, but needed specialized functions to best serve its customers. They hired Trineo to help. Trineo used Salesforce's PaaS to create customized applications that enabled Menumate to enhance the functionality of their Salesforce CRM data. Now, the Menumate staff can print freight labels, track perishable goods, and update customer information—none of which are functions built into the SaaS CRM.

Because PaaS lies atop an IaaS, functions such as Autoscale and Monitoring are already built into a provider's cloud. This makes PaaS particularly appealing for enterprises that may suddenly experience tremendous and unexpected growth in popularity. In one case, a cloud with PaaS enabled the media company Al Jazeera to react to world events with no significant downtime. In the first months of 2011, as several North African nations experienced protests and revolutions, Al Jazeera had reporters throughout the region. During the upheavals in Egypt, web traffic on Al Jazeera's Internet pages rose by 1,000 percent. According to cloud computing and infrastructure specialist Sanjay Srivastava:

> With a traditional hosting service hopelessly unable to handle the traffic surge, Al Jazeera moved its site to a PaaS service. It thus obtained an elastic number

of web-server platforms that grew and shrunk in response to traffic.

In allowing server numbers to increase with demand, PaaS eradicated Al Jazeera's problems in responding to changes in traffic. The speed with which Al Jazeera gained this capability was astounding, achieved with no upfront expenditure and little (if any) additional manpower.[26]

One Percent but Growing

Al Jazeera's success story shows the benefits of a PaaS strategy. Currently, however, PaaS remains an underutilized segment of the stack; a 2012 study by the information and technology research firm Gartner, Inc. found that the PaaS market represented only 1 percent of the total cloud services market. Gartner also noted that PaaS represents a small but growing field. Although less money is spent on PaaS than on SaaS and IaaS, businesses worldwide spent approximately $1.2 billion on PaaS in 2012, out of an estimated $109 billion

A screenshot of the Al Jazeera website shows part of its coverage from May 2, 2011. Earlier that year, when web traffic to the site increased by 1,000 percent, it met the new demand by switching to a PaaS service.

spent on cloud computing in general. The study noted that PaaS revenue increased from $900 million in 2011, and was expected to increase to $2.9 billion by 2016; by that time, total cloud computing revenue is estimated to be $207 billion.

Part of the reason that PaaS revenue lags behind SaaS and IaaS may be because it was the last layer of the stack to be introduced. Perhaps it has to deal with confusion over what platform means in its name. Kepes theorizes that "PaaS is where cloud [in general] was six years ago. . . . If you know exactly how you're going to build, the sort of architectural paradigm you want to use, then find a Platform as a Service that fits that and you're probably going to be better off. But most people aren't at that point yet."[27]

As businesses continue to consider how best to move to the cloud, and to debate whether they need a public, private, or hybrid cloud model, consumers continue to use the Internet as never before. Their interests drive traffic to sites both old and young, create new trends in entertainment and service, and look to access the Web from everywhere. They look to create, expand, and cultivate contacts in new and different ways without the need for specialized equipment. The evolving world of the social cloud enables them to do just that.

CHAPTER 3

The Social Cloud

The rise of Web 2.0 in the early twenty-first century led to an unprecedented number of individuals around the world sharing their opinions about everything from local, national, and international politics to the latest pop stars. The growth of social media led to websites for music enthusiasts, environmentalists, educators, followers of particular political parties or philosophies, and much more. World Wide Web users share jokes, viral videos, and memes from home, work, and, increasingly, from Internet-connected mobile phones.

All of this Internet traffic needs to access information on websites' servers. Many sites are moving from physical servers in a data center to virtual servers in the cloud. Others are avoiding purchasing physical infrastructure altogether and using the cloud from the beginning. Their use of cloud computing has led to a convergence with Web 2.0 that continues to shape the future of communication, collaboration, and creativity both on and off the Internet. One preferred method is via short-form bursts of information called microblogging.

Microblogging in the Cloud

Microblogs provide a ready means of sharing views across the web in a compact format. Sites such as Twitter, Facebook, and Blogger are hallmarks of this type of social media. Newer sites such as Tumblr, Instagram, and Pinterest have carved niches of their own. Both established sites and newcomers enable users to communicate and collaborate via the cloud without specialized software or hardware. Users can share stories, photos, and videos from a variety of file formats and from a variety of operating systems, and can see content from their contacts and from their interests, such as bands, artists, comedians, and more.

Some microblogging content is only visible to a select group. Social media sites such as Facebook and Google+ enable users to restrict who sees their content. Others, such as Tumblr and Twitter, have content that is accessible to all. Businesses and organizations around the world have taken advantage of these new media forms to share milestones, upcoming events, sales, new products, and more. Some firms are large enough to have employees whose job is to manage these accounts; others empower all employees to create and post content.

Fashion design company Kenneth Cole discovered that this last method can lead to unintended consequences. Employees generally used the company Twitter account to promote their product line, but in February 2011, when Egypt was undergoing a revolution, someone at Kenneth Cole posted: "Millions are in uproar in #Cairo. Rumor is they heard our new spring collection is now available online...."[28] On Twitter, users insert the "#" character before a word or a phrase of their choice to create a searchable term called a hashtag. The hashtag #Cairo had been helping Twitter users follow developments in Egypt's capital. Other microbloggers expressed dismay over what they perceived as a tasteless attempt to link the political upheaval with a line of fashion. The Kenneth Cole company eventually tweeted an apology.

The misuse of #Cairo temporarily derailed the flow of information from microbloggers uploading vital news and information to the cloud. Twitter users quickly created other hashtags directly related to the Kenneth Cole tweet, giving those who wished to comment on the issue a way to do so without interrupting the news and information related to the events in Egypt.

Hashtags for Activism

Activists around the world recognize that microblogging via Twitter can help bring attention to their causes. They use it to share links, to promote issues, and to create meetings and protests. For example, in December 2012, when the Michigan State Legislature unexpectedly introduced controversial labor relations bills, pro-union advocates took to Twitter to organize protests, using the hashtag #righttowork. Once the story became national news, the newspaper in the state capital, the *Lansing State Journal,* tweeted its stories with the simpler hashtag #Michigan.

Microbloggers also create hashtags from catchphrases. During the 2012 U.S. presidential campaign, Republican Party nominee Mitt Romney discussed that as governor of Massachusetts he wanted to recruit more females to his cabinet, saying, "I went to a number of women's groups and

Twitter messages are displayed on huge screens at the 2012 Republican National Convention. Social media platforms such as Twitter are used throughout the world for political purposes.

said, 'Can you help us find folks,' and they brought us whole binders full of women."[29] The phrase "binders full of women" became a hashtag almost instantly and, within minutes, had led to a variety of memes and pages on Facebook and Tumblr.

Few tweets or hashtags become national or international news. Most microblog content is intended for far smaller circles. Yet, it is one of the hallmarks of cloud computing—virtually unlimited offsite storage—that enables users of social media to enjoy and share their pastimes and passions with friends and family.

The Social Network Cloud

Cloud-based social networks are used by millions of people around the world to keep in touch with friends and family. Individuals can share photos of gatherings around a campfire in a park or videos of performances of their favorite musicians. The social networks' application programming interfaces, or APIs, effectively convert multiple file formats into images that everyone can enjoy.

Some individuals, however, choose to take advantage of the cloud for more individual enrichment. Internet-based mobile phone applications, or apps, provide a wide range of opportunities for people to pursue hobbies and interests on their own, such as creating an exercise routine. Many of these cloud-based apps are still platform-dependent; some will work only on Apple's iOS or on Google's Android operating systems. But they enable the user to track their fitness progress and chart their success. For example, Strava.com caters to bicyclists; the site's app interfaces with the GPS function on a cyclist's mobile phone to determine how far he or she has ridden during each workout. It also enables the cyclist to download a range of challenging rides in the local area submitted by other enthusiasts.

Sharing personal news via a social network is a commonplace activity. Sharing personal workout success thanks to a certain app, however, may seem like an advertisement for the particular exercise program. In fact, businesses count on the reviews in such posts to drive business to their apps or

A cyclist inputs data into a smartphone. Fitness apps such as Strava use social media tools on the cloud.

other products. Facebook, YouTube, and other outlets provide these businesses with a cost-effective means of spreading the word about brands and products. Yet, in a world that is increasingly connected to the cloud, a post in one place can lead to unexpected consequences elsewhere.

"The Worst Thing You Could Possibly Do"

In early 2013, the restaurant chain Applebee's became embroiled in a widely publicized controversy that began with a photo shared on the cloud-based citizen-journalism site Reddit.com. On Tuesday, January 29, Chelsea Welch, a server at one of its St. Louis-area restaurants, snapped a photo of a meal receipt received by one of her colleagues who had served a large party of customers, led by a local pastor. The pastor refused to pay the 18 percent tip automatically generated for large groups, noting on the receipt

Application Programming Interfaces

The application programming interface (API) plays an important part in cloud computing. An API is a set of programming instructions that facilitates communication between software applications without user input. In cloud computing, where there is often a mix of applications hosted onsite and offsite, this communication is essential. One provider of API hosting even went so far as to claim, "Without APIs, there is no cloud computing."[1]

As cloud computing has grown, cloud computing providers such as Amazon, Google, and Microsoft have continued to offer new features to stay competitive. This brings more APIs into play as an evolving part of the cloud computing landscape. Mike Denning, security general manager of CA Technologies, says:

> We use APIs every day, whether accessing flight data from our mobile device, using Google Maps from a hotel website or making payments online. There are billions of API calls a day and that number is going to increase with the proliferation of smart devices, ranging from vehicles, meters, TVs and other devices, as they start interacting over APIs.[2]

1. Mashery. "APIs the Key to a Thriving Cloud." Readwrite.com, February, 26, 2009. http://readwrite.com/2009/02/26/mashery_apis_the_key_to_a_thriving _cloud#awesm=~oz9CRhCNj4t263.

2. CA Technologies. "CA Technologies to Acquire Privately-Held Layer 7 Technologies, a Leader in API Management and Security." Press release, April 22, 2013. www.ca.com/us/news/press-releases/na/2013/ca-technologies-to-acquire-privately-held-layer-7-technologies.aspx.

that she contributed only 10 percent to her church. Welch uploaded the image to Reddit "because I thought other users would find it entertaining." She said she found the pastor's note "insulting, but it was also comical."[30] The image of the receipt, which included the pastor's signature, went viral. Reddit users attempted to decipher the signature and then scoured the Internet to ascertain the pastor's identity. They posted dozens of messages on the Reddit page with links to web addresses and Facebook profiles, asking Welch to confirm the pastor's identity. She refused to help, saying she didn't want to get the woman in trouble.

The discussion might have stayed within the Reddit community except that a Reddit reader shared it with *The Consumerist,* the blog of the nonprofit advocacy group Consumer Reports. They interviewed Welch later that day, and her story was taken up by other media outlets. When the pastor discovered that her note was everywhere online, she complained to Applebee's. The restaurant fired Welch on January 31 for violating a policy of sharing customer information.

The story did not end there. As news of Welch's firing spread on February 1, the receipt's image became the centerpiece of hundreds of blog posts and media articles. It also prompted thousands of comments on Applebee's Facebook wall, protesting her dismissal. The corporation's four-person social media team initially addressed the issue by posting the corporate policy statement about sharing customer information, but the comments kept coming—at more than a thousand an hour overnight into February 2. Some posters accused Applebee's team of deleting posts and blocking people from making further comments. That made matters even worse. By 3:00 a.m., the team was replying to each post by cutting and pasting the policy statement. Finally, after more than forty thousand responses to their posts and replies, they disabled user comments. The responses disappeared from their Facebook wall on the morning of February 2. Travis Mayfield, of media advertising consultancy Fisher Interactive Networks, said, "That was a terrible idea. It seemed like they were deleting posts, which is the worst thing you could possibly do."[31] Crisis management expert Louis Richmond added, "It's very complicated to respond to negative social media. We tell our [public relations] clients to respond, but don't criticize. And never hide posts because people see that as censorship."[32]

Opportunities to Engage Are Everywhere

The five days of coverage related to the Applebee's incident provided an interesting lesson in cloud-based social media. Welch discovered that sharing anything in the cloud can bring unintended consequences, and Applebee's learned that their reactions to the backlash needed scrutiny. An Applebee's spokesman told a reporter that they would "need to have a conversation"[33] within the company about their choice to turn off the comment feature. William Ward, professor of social media at Syracuse University, urges organizations in such circumstances to be prepared for social media disasters, because the wrong response can make matters worse. "You need to have internal policies and procedures on how to handle something like this. If you address the negative comments in a positive way, it's an opportunity to show people you're listening. You may actually create a more loyal customer or fan just from engaging with them the right way."[34]

One example of an organization listening to and engaging with their customers comes from Gatwick Airport, outside London, England. In July 2012, Gatwick partnered with SoundCloud, the world's largest community of artists, bands, podcasters, and creators of music and audio. In order to help keep families with young children entertained while waiting for their flights, Gatwick's communications team posted a series of fairy tales, such as *Sleeping Beauty* and *The Ugly Duckling,* to their SoundCloud channel. Walker Books, an independent British publisher, later enhanced the channel by donating a selection of children's audio books. Zoe Baker, a spokesperson for Gatwick, said the initiative was designed to "embrace social communities and enhance a passenger's journey as they pass through the airport."[35]

The Gatwick initiative demonstrates an innovative method to bring cloud-based content to a new audience. Airline passengers may decide to return to Gatwick for future flights, bringing more business to the airport; they may take time to explore SoundCloud further, discovering its wide variety of science podcasts, political commentary, and comedy performances. SoundCloud also provides an opportunity for aspiring and established musicians to share their compositions in the cloud.

Music from the Cloud

While some musicians are willing to share their music on the Internet, others may not be so accommodating. Music on the Internet has been a contentious matter for many years. Some services, such as Napster, were forced to shut down because their users made illegal copies of copyrighted music, which meant that the performers did not receive royalties they were due. Some artists, such as Kid Rock and AC/DC, resisted licensing their music for downloads for many years before reaching agreements with music giant iTunes. Yet, dedicated fans were often able to find copies of their favorite artists' music in the cloud, usually through YouTube.

YouTube is the world's most popular site for sharing videos. The site's terms of use clearly state that whoever uploads a video must have ownership of the content or have copyright permission to share it. However, individuals continue to create short films that include copyrighted music or video clips and upload them to YouTube's cloud. Additionally, with the increased functionality of Internet-connected smartphones, concert-goers often record events and post clips to YouTube before the concert ends.

Not all music in the cloud is there illegally, of course. Enthusiasts have their choice of many types of music providers where they can listen to songs for which companies have purchased performance rights. Some providers, such as Pandora, Last.fm, and iHeart Radio, are available free of charge and require no special software installation. These services are very popular: According to Manual Roig-Franzia of the *Washington Post,* in March 2013 Pandora had "more than 69 million users listening to more than 1.5 billion hours of music in a month," and could be found "embedded into the dashboard of 80 or so new car models."[36]

These free services are supported by advertisements, placed on the music services' websites and in between songs.

Listeners wishing to avoid such interruptions can pay for subscriptions to sites such as Rdio, Spotify, and iTunes. These services not only stream from cloud servers, but also enable subscribers to choose specific bands or songs for their playlists. John-Scott Dixon of *Cloud Magazine* prefers Rdio because it has a mobile phone app available for a wide variety of devices and because it "does a crazy, great job of recommending new music at every step based on my Rdio history combined with my Facebook history. . . . But what has tipped me in favor of Rdio, is the ability to create a network of people based on similar musical tastes and see what's popular across that group."[37] For many music enthusiasts, listening to streaming music from cloud-based servers is adequate for their entertainment needs. Others have greater requirements.

Channeling Musical Creativity

The cloud provides opportunities for musicians to collaborate and share as never before. SoundCloud enables both amateur and professional musicians an outlet for their compositions. Rocky Mountain Mike is a musician who plays guitar, keyboards, mandolin, and more, and collaborates with other musicians across the United States to create musical parodies. He says, "I'll have them record either .wav or .mp3 files along to a pre-recorded [melody]," which he then mixes with recording software and then uploads to his SoundCloud channel. He prefers SoundCloud over YouTube "because you don't have to produce any video to go with it, and it uploads about a hundred times faster."[38]

Rocky Mountain Mike has more than eight hundred followers on SoundCloud, where he has posted nearly three hundred musical and political satires. His channel provides an outlet for his creativity, but music is not his full-time occupation. On the other hand, professional musicians use SoundCloud to share their latest performances, remastered mixes, and personal thoughts on touring, meeting

SoundCloud is an online audio distribution platform based in Germany with more than 10 million users.

fans, social media, and more. SoundCloud appeals to a wide range of listeners: In mid-2013, country singer Carrie Underwood had nearly one hundred thousand followers and boy band One Direction had more than seven hundred thousand.

In many instances, professional musicians use Sound-Cloud to share previews of performances. This practice challenges the cloud-based listening experience, as the fan either has to upgrade to a paid subscription or purchase the track to hear the full selection. An additional challenge to enjoying cloud-based music, either from a service or of a personal collection, comes with the challenge of connectivity. An Internet connection with inadequate bandwidth or a weak signal will diminish the musical experience. But as more and more households use high-speed access to the web, cloud-based content is now more than just music. Streaming television and video create new options for home entertainment.

Entertainment in the Cloud

The world of home entertainment continues to evolve. A growing number of American viewers are cancelling their cable or satellite TV subscriptions in favor of watching online content through their traditional television sets or portable electronic devices. Many in these households opt for streaming content, which uses a high-speed broadband or WiFi connection to bring video to viewers without needing to download large video files.

To enjoy streaming content, such as a film or a TV show, the consumer visits the website of a content provider, such as Netflix, Hulu, Apple TV, or Amazon, and selects a program. The video is then sent via the Internet connection to his or her particular device for viewing, and can then be relayed by a wired or wireless connection to home theater equipment. The content remains on the provider's cloud, and the consumer does not need high-capacity storage in order to watch it.

Streaming is gaining in popularity among American viewers, particularly those in their twenties and thirties. Subscriptions to streaming services continue to rise. For example, in the first three months of 2013, Netflix signed up more than 2 million new subscribers; by the end of March, the company had 29 million streaming customers in the United States and 7 million overseas. Yet streaming is not for everyone, as technological challenges may diminish the streaming experience. Like every new technology, it has its pros and cons.

Streaming Pros and Cons

Streaming advocates say that the costs connected with streaming are lower, as subscription costs are generally less than a cable or satellite television bill. They maintain that streaming providers have a larger menu of nontraditional programming, such as international films, than can be found via American television providers. Proponents such as Len Markidan, a twenty-six-year-old marketing consultant based in San Francisco, say that streaming provides them with the content they want, when they want, regardless of location. Markidan spends 40 percent of his time traveling on business and takes his Apple MacBook Pro and iPad with him. His devices enable him to watch his favorite television programs by streaming them to his laptop. He says, "For a lot of people my age and a lot of people in general, the way we consume entertainment at home is changing. I no longer have a cable subscription—the way I watch entertainment at home is the same way I watch it on the road. I have a Hulu subscription, Amazon Prime and Netflix."[39]

Streaming has some drawbacks, too. It uses a large amount of bandwidth, which can limit Internet access for other family members, or which may lead to overage charges. Not all content found on a cable or satellite system is in the cloud; for example, ESPN's sports coverage is not available for streaming. Additionally, first-run episodes of some television series may take up to a year to be streamed.

For many, the advantages outweigh the disadvantages. The number of American households that no longer

A woman watches a movie streaming on a tablet while a second movie plays on a large-screen monitor. Cloud-based movie streaming services are revolutionizing entertainment options for consumers.

subscribe to satellite or cable services continues to rise. In 2007, there were 2 million of these "zero TV" residences in the United States; by 2012, the number had more than doubled to 5 million.

In addition to television and film content streamed online, many consumers also choose to stream video game content to their personal devices.

"We Went from 1 Million to 9 Million in a Couple of Months"

Video gaming has grown in popularity in the first years of the twenty-first century. It is the fastest-growing media industry; by 2011, sales revenues from video games were more than double those from the recorded music industry. The growth of cloud computing is leading to more opportunities, for both providers and video game enthusiasts alike, due to the cloud's flexible storage and scalability options and its cross-platform availability. In just a few short years, computer-based gaming has transformed from a solitary activity requiring specialized programming and equipment to a community-based experience, involving players from around the world.

Placing games in the cloud has benefitted both provider and gamer. By using cloud-based virtual servers, providers can easily scale up to meet demand. For example, after *Fruit Ninja Frenzy*, a game created by Australian developer Halfbrick, debuted on Facebook, user numbers went from hundreds of thousands to millions. According to Halfbrick's executive producer Dale Freya, "At one point Facebook did a promotion on the game, and we weren't even aware of it. The game went from 1 million active monthly users to about 9 million in the course of a couple of months."[40] However, since they were using Amazon Web Services (AWS) to host the game, they were able to scale up their services to accommodate the increased popularity.

Cloud-based gaming enables gamers to log on and play at any time, even during peak demand hours. Providers that relied on in-house server infrastructure often had trouble meeting demand; in one case, players hoping to play an update to the popular *Team Fortress 2* shortly after its 2012 release often had to wait up to thirty minutes for an available server. Cloud-based games also eliminate the need for downloading and storing a game locally, meaning players can participate in more than one game at a time.

The proliferation of mobile phones and other handheld devices has also encouraged game developers to consider the cloud. Major game makers including Electronic Arts (EA), Microsoft, Nintendo, and Sony are migrating their content to cloud environments and creating content that gamers can play on one device, pause, and then continue playing on another. EA's president Frank Gibeau points to their international soccer game *FIFA*, which is available across twelve different gaming environments. "*FIFA* fans can check their standings on their mobile device or tablet, manipulate their teams on Facebook or play an immersive game of *FIFA* on their PC or console. Everything is connected so the user can pick up just where they left off from anywhere."[41]

Gaming from Anywhere

EA's FIFA is one example of a cloud-based game that can be played from almost anywhere and on multiple types of devices. So far, however, cloud-based gaming has been less popular than console-based or downloaded games played over the Internet. In mid-2012, the total number of subscribers to the two leading cloud-based gaming companies was far less than some individual games that are available for download or purchase. The two companies, OnLive and Gaikai, had an estimated 2 million subscribers between them; by contrast, the downloadable online game *World of Warcraft* had more than 10 million subscribers.

This may give the impression that cloud-based gaming has a limited future. Certainly, the massive downsizing at OnLive in August 2012 might support that premise; more than 50 percent of the company's 200 employees were laid off. But electronics giant Sony may feel otherwise, because it purchased Gaikai for $380 million that same year. Gaikai's technology was integrated into Sony's PlayStation 4, enabling players to stream portions of their games online, so other users could watch. Another company that would disagree is San Francisco-based Twitch, which enables gamers to broadcast via their streaming feed as they play. Twitch had more than 28 million unique visitors in February 2013, just eighteen months after its debut.

Twitch does not develop any of the content they stream; instead, they work with developers to create functions within their games to connect with Twitch for a more social experience. Playing a video game with others to achieve a certain goal is not new; massive multiplayer online role-playing

PlayStation 4 is enabled for cloud-based streaming content, including Twitch. During the system's launch event in New York City, a video gamer plays on a remote device with the game projected on a building facade.

Cloud-Based Gaming May Reduce Piracy

One of the burning issues in video gaming is piracy. A video game pirate may steal some or all of the content from a particular game and then modify the content in order to publish a similar product. Such theft is rampant in international markets. For example, the popular game *Angry Birds* was one of the most pirated games in China during 2011.

Game developers, of course, would like to see an end to piracy, because it would reduce illegal copies and would ensure that customers are purchasing legitimate versions. One potential avenue for reducing piracy is moving gaming to the cloud.

In cloud-based gaming, a game is streamed like a YouTube video to a computer or other electronic device. This means that the game will only exist in the cloud; with no hard copies available, industry experts believe it will be almost impossible for piracy to continue.

Currently, a limited number of games are available in the cloud, but one provider believes that gaming will exist only in the cloud in just a few years. Steve Perlman, CEO of game provider OnLive, says, "We'll be there in 10 years—if that."

Quoted in Matthew Lynley. "Cloud-Based Video Games Will Put Pirates Out of Business." *VentureBeat,* July 14, 2011. venturebeat.com/2011/07/14/cloud-gaming-piracy.

games such as *World of Warcraft* and *Call of Duty* have been popular for years. Yet, fully streamed versions of these games are still not a reality, as cloud-based gaming continues to mature.

It is important to remember that content in the cloud is not merely for entertainment. Educators around the world are discovering the cloud provides amazing new opportunities to create content and to collaborate with students and colleagues as never before.

New Educational Environments

Cloud computing provides opportunities for more than just business and entertainment. Students and educators are using the cloud for a wide variety of innovative purposes, thereby expanding students' expertise with technology and their knowledge of the world around them. Many students are already accustomed to receiving and submitting homework assignments through the Internet. But in cases in which students still need to access the school's server, they can encounter problems during busy periods. Larry Steinke, technology director of Saint Francis High School in Mountain View, California, says that in-house infrastructure is particularly vulnerable "if you have students using computer labs where important files and work can easily become lost—and are needed right away at finals time."[42]

The cloud is helpful in this type of situation. For example, teachers at Hobart Middle School in Hobart, Indiana, post their lessons and assignments through Google Apps, which provides e-mail services, file sharing, peer-review features, and administrative controls. The SaaS program suite enables the students to interact through their classroom laptops or other mobile devices, and enables the educators to keep track of their students' participation. Matt Whiteman, an eighth grade social studies teacher, uses the cloud to help his students create web pages to showcase their assignments through digital portfolios and to develop blogs to debate questions posed in class. He believes that technology is an integral part of life and that students need to be able to use computers and other devices in order to succeed in college and in their jobs. He adds, "This generation needs to be excited about technology and what it can do."[43]

One of the ways educators are helping their students become excited is through the development of personal learning environments. The teachers set a series of expectations and compulsory outcomes to ensure that the students meet all applicable education requirements, and then let the students determine how they can go about satisfying the expectations. The students use a variety of electronic devices, including laptops, tablets, and smartphones, to work with the instructors and each other to investigate

topics and to complete assignments, storing their drafts, sources, and web-links in the cloud. The result is often a mix of SaaS-based websites, such as wikis or blogs, personalized programs, and customized or newly developed apps created by the students to demonstrate their understanding of the assignment. Students also share their creations via public sites such as YouTube or SoundCloud, or by specialized sites such as VoiceThread, which allows students and teachers to integrate classroom content, assignments, photographs, and videos, and to share them worldwide if they choose.

For the educator, having the students' projects in the cloud enables them to track overall progress and to provide active coaching in skills such as writing and grammar. Education in the cloud, however, is not limited to SaaS-based applications in the classroom. School districts are also discovering the benefit of IaaS for their needs.

Students in Wellsville, New York, follow a lesson using computer tablets in 2013. Schools and educators have developed personal learning environments and other cloud-based tools for students using cloud-based services.

IaaS Goes to School

As in the world of business, IaaS in the world of education takes place behind the scenes. Students and educators may not be aware that their networks are IaaS-based, but school district IT departments are discovering that deploying IaaS can have definite benefits for the schools they represent.

IT professionals can deploy multiple operating system instances to meet the demands of students and educators as well as administrative and support staff. For example, education IT staff can use IaaS to create a virtual private network (VPN) that mixes onsite and cloud infrastructure and has Internet addresses that are accessible even in the event of a hardware failure. Dian Schaffhauser, writing for

THE Journal, notes that this type of network can add an important layer of security for educational institutions in two ways: "First, [virtual servers] and cloud services within a virtual network can do simple communication without having to go through a public IP address. Second, [virtual servers] outside of the virtual network can't connect to or even identify services hosted within the network."[44]

Within this VPN, schools can safeguard valuable information. This includes students' grades, contact information, and disciplinary records, and staff employment histories and pension records. IT staff can build an e-mail system or a social network within such a VPN, providing a secure means of communication between individuals—student to student, student to educator, and educator to educator. Additionally, IaaS providers, such as Microsoft and Google, offer collaboration tools, enabling students to work together within the network on a common platform.

It is important to note, however, that a school's decision to move from an in-house server infrastructure to cloud computing requires more study than a business considering a similar situation. Schools, colleges, and universities have a radically different type of business model. Public K-12 schools are funded by taxes paid by local citizens and revenues generated by local cities and towns. State colleges and universities receive their funding from state legislatures. Private schools and universities raise money through tuition, grants, donations, and more. Each is subject to a variety of state, local, and federal regulations concerning the availability and security of student and employee information. Therefore, moving to the cloud requires careful study and consideration of many different factors, including cost, security, and who will be responsible for all that data.

CHAPTER 4

Downtime and Security in the Cloud

It is difficult to imagine the twenty-first century without our personal computers. Millions of people around the world use them to store everything from baby photos to complex legal documents. Organizations large and small rely on them on a daily basis to communicate and collaborate with members, other groups, and businesses around the world.

The field of cloud computing has brought new choices to these computer users. Well-educated consumers are in the best position to make an informed decision about the direction of their computing future. One of the questions to consider is the specter of downtime. If a data center's server fails, websites and other vital information, such as a company's e-mail or personnel records, may become inaccessible. Downtime occurs in both traditional and cloud-based operations. Businesses considering a move to the cloud must evaluate what each cloud provider offers as well as the potential cloud provider's track record, including previous instances of downtime. Having data in the cloud is worthless if it is inaccessible.

Outages and Downtime

As with many new technologies, cloud computing attracts little attention from everyday news coverage unless something extraordinary occurs. One such incident happened on December 24, 2012. Amazon Web Services' (AWS) cloud-based servers run websites across the globe, and most visitors to these sites never notice who is hosting the data they access until something goes wrong. On Christmas Eve, something went wrong and people noticed. The movie provider Netflix experienced significant downtime when it was unavailable for most of the day. Amazon's own streaming service, Amazon Prime, experienced briefer interruptions. Social media sites filled with complaints over the outages. AWS issued a statement on its website indicating that it had traced the problem to its load balancing system at a data center in Ashburn, Virginia, and that it had completely fixed the problem by Christmas Day. This was the same data center that had experienced problems twice earlier that year. An outage in June was blamed on an electrical storm, taking Netflix, Pinterest, Instagram, and other sites offline for hours. Four months later, an outage blamed on "degraded performance"[45] took out Foursquare, Reddit, and Heroku.

Such downtime is inconvenient for the World Wide Web user, but it means lost revenue for the cloud customer. For example, an AWS outage in January 2013 affected parent company Amazon's main website; the site was down for forty-nine minutes, resulting in an estimated $4 million in lost sales. Google and Microsoft both experienced outages in March 2013. These events were well-publicized but temporary and, according to most observers, did not likely affect the providers adversely. James McQuivey, an analyst for Forrester Research, said that companies "are going to say, 'Gee, Amazon, what's going on?' But in reality . . . I don't see them getting that upset about it."[46] He felt that few businesses were likely to leave AWS because it continued to offer new services and lower costs. Technology writer Barb Darrow agreed, but also ventured that "issues like this one can only help AWS rivals in the OpenStack [open source] community—Rackspace, Hewlett-Packard et al. that are trying to position their cloud services as options with better service and support, if not the same huge scale as AWS."[47] As *InfoWorld*'s David Linthicum puts it, "It always comes down to dollars and cents."[48]

Protection Is Essential

The issue of dollars and cents sometimes takes a backseat to the security of gigabytes and terabytes. For many company executives, the potential loss of revenue from a cloud provider outage pales to the loss of the business itself through a security breach. According to John Onwamba, a cloud technology writer, a global study by IBM in 2012 that involved more than five hundred IT managers showed that "50% feared data breaches [and] another 23% fear[ed] that cloud computing threatens corporate security."[49]

All of this concern means that customers need to thoroughly investigate the cloud providers' methods for protecting both the data center's infrastructure and the data center's contents. Unfortunately, according to Steve Durbin, an executive vice president at Information Security Forum:

> In the rush to adopt cloud services and realize the potential savings they may give . . . companies are concentrating on the functionality of the cloud services and failing to ask questions about the way cloud providers deliver security across their services or how that security can be checked.
>
> This happens when companies assume that because cloud service providers service multiple companies, they have a larger security department and stronger policies, processes, and procedures.[50]

In addition to asking questions about a cloud provider's security methods, potential cloud customers also need to investigate if their division, corporation, or other governing body already has security guidelines in place. Moving to the cloud without understanding and complying with these guidelines can lead to problems both inside and outside the organization.

"Weaknesses Have Impeded the Agency"

Cloud security guidelines vary from organization to organization. Small to medium-sized businesses, or SMBs, may rely on in-house or outside IT professionals to assess their security needs. Their policies need only address their presence in the cloud. However, when a U.S. government agency considers moving to the cloud, it needs to conform to a set of standards called the Federal Risk and Authorization Management Program, or FedRAMP. FedRAMP provides a government-wide and standardized approach to cloud security assessment, authorization, and continuous monitoring, and it is the responsibility of the General Accounting Office (GAO) to ensure that all federal agencies are complying with it. In July 2013, the GAO released a report that assessed the space agency NASA's use of the cloud. While noting that NASA was helping to lead the U.S. government's move to the cloud, the GAO found several shortcomings regarding those efforts.

This was not the first time NASA's use of the cloud was in the news. Multiple media sources had reported in 2012 that NASA's Jet Propulsion Laboratory (JPL) had selected AWS to publicize the mission of *Curiosity,* the new Mars rover. Khawaja Shams, JPL's manager for data services, noted that they partnered with AWS to "cost effectively expand the computational horsepower we have at our disposal," which would allow them to capture, store, and share data and images from the mission. JPL said, "Cloud computing is giving us that opportunity."[51] JPL also worked with AWS to create a dedicated website, mars.jpl.nasa.gov, which was solely for content associated with the rover's mission. According to Amit Chowdhry, a technology reporter, "Using AWS, NASA was able to build a scalable web infrastructure in only 2-3 weeks instead of months."[52] Earlier NASA cloud endeavors led to partnerships with other cloud providers, including Microsoft and Google. Shams said that with each new project, JPL evaluates providers "to find the right cloud for the right job."[53]

Unfortunately, according to the GAO report, NASA had not met FedRAMP security guidelines while using these public cloud services. In some cases, data had been moved to public clouds without the knowledge or consent of the agency's Office of the Chief Information Officer; in one case, data had been stored on a public cloud for two years without authorization. The report stated, "We found that weaknesses in NASA's IT governance and risk management

Data collected by NASA's Mars rover Curiosity—seen in a self-portrait from the planet's surface—is available to research and educational users through the AWS cloud.

practices have impeded the Agency from fully realizing the benefits of cloud computing and potentially put NASA systems and data stored in the cloud at risk."[54]

The report concluded with several recommendations, including the establishment of a cloud computing program management office to strengthen oversight and compliance with FedRAMP. FedRAMP standards, of course, do not apply to SMBs or other commercial enterprises. These private businesses do, however, have a way to ensure that their cloud provider meets their security needs. The best way customers interested in cloud computing services can ensure that security measures are handled to their specifications is through the service-level agreement.

The SLA

The service-level agreement (SLA) is a negotiated contract between customer and provider for cloud computing services. Kaiser Wahab is a media and technology attorney based in New York, New York, who blogs about cloud services and the law. He points out that when it comes to agreements between customers and providers, "there is no template SLA and each cloud solution vendor is unique."[55]

Wahab notes that the best SLA needs to cover much more than pricing. It should outline the specific security measures the provider uses to ensure customer data protection and privacy; how the provider complies with local, state, and governmental regulations about data security; and should provide the customer with the ability to audit the provider's security practices and procedures on an annual basis. The SLA should also cover security breaches, outlining how they will be handled and by which party of the contract.

Jerry Irvine is the chief information officer of Prescient Solutions and a member of the National Cyber Security Task Force. He points out that establishing who is responsible for security is essential in an effective SLA. In some cases, cloud providers may hire an outside firm to provide high levels of security that are beyond their expertise. Irvine notes that the security services of these third parties may not be covered in the standard SLA that the provider shares with the customer. He says, "You have to require the service provider to maintain specific security functions, document security tasks, and provide copies of all security policies and practices as well as security reports."[56] And because one of the major selling points of working in the cloud is the ability to access data anywhere online, the provider needs to accurately address who can access the data and how it will be secured. This often depends on which level of the stack the customer uses.

Securing Access and Backup

Cloud customers must understand that while data access, protection, and privacy often depend on which layer of the stack is being used, they are always responsible for controlling access to the applications. This means, for example, an SMB running a SaaS-based CRM application must establish controls that restrict which employees can log on to the app and access its sensitive customer information. With SaaS, the consumer does not manage or control the network, the servers, storage, or the capabilities of the applications. Jay

Inside a Data Center

Cloud providers are zealous about the security of their data centers. In October 2012, however, Google briefly lifted the veil on its operations by granting several reporters access to its data center in Lenoir, North Carolina. The reporters received a firsthand look at the measures that the computing giant takes to safeguard the facility and the data.

The site itself is heavily guarded and patrolled; access barriers designed to disable vehicles are present at every entrance. Inside the perimeter, video cameras monitor activity, and, inside the building, key card security and biometric retina scanning restrict access to sensitive areas including the servers.

When *CBS This Morning*'s Michelle Miller visited, Google had 55,200 servers operating in the server room. The room itself was 77°F (25°C); the narrow space between the racks was 120°F (49°C). *Wired* magazine's Steven Levy described the room during his visit:

> All the cables and plugs are in front. . . . Each server has a sticker with a code that identifies its exact address, useful if something goes wrong. The servers have thick black batteries alongside. . . . Blue lights twinkle, indicating . . . what? A web search? Someone's Gmail message? . . . It could be anything.

Steven Levy. "Google Throws Open Doors to Its Top-Secret Data Center." *Wired*, October 17, 2012. www.wired.com/wiredenterprise/2012/10/ff-inside-google-data-center/all.

Heiser, an analyst at market research firm Gartner, notes that "security responsibilities [with SaaS applications] are almost entirely up to the vendor. If the vendor doesn't encrypt data, it's not encrypted. If there isn't any activity monitoring, you won't get any."[57]

But SaaS is only part of "the stack." Businesses desiring more security from those inside and outside their firm should investigate PaaS and IaaS. Mike Kavis, founder of Kavis Technology

Consulting, says, "As you go from SaaS to PaaS and IaaS, the level of control you have over security changes."[58] PaaS offers more control over security than SaaS. As with SaaS, customers have no control over the security of the cloud infrastructure, but with PaaS, they can determine the level of control over the apps they deploy. PaaS deployments also provide the customer with the opportunity to supplement built-in security programs by deploying their own measures that ensure the protection of their apps, their APIs, and authentication protocols. At the bottom of the stack, the IaaS vendor provides few integrated security capabilities beyond protecting the server infrastructure. This means that the customer has complete control over how much security to install. Chris Barber is chief information officer at American LegalNet, which provides technology solutions to courthouse workplaces. He believes that the multiple options available with IaaS may lead to server and hypervisor vulnerabilities: "Since you have multiple users on a single physical box, there may be a security vulnerability that one user could somehow access another user's virtual machine."[59] It is, therefore, essential that users secure the operating systems they deploy, along with the apps and content, with effective access controls and firewalls.

Managing and securing cloud-based data also includes creating backups. Having a backup of cloud-based data will help an organization in case a provider has an outage. One option is to hire a third-party vendor to manage this task. For example, a company called Backupify creates backups of information from a variety of SaaS-based applications, such as Salesforce and Google Apps. Another option is to create an identical server instance within the cloud provider's infrastructure, or with another provider, to serve as a backup. Jim Reavis is the executive director of the Cloud Security Alliance (CSA), a nonprofit organization that partners with industry members worldwide to promote and provide education for effective cloud computing security. He notes that the CSA stores its data with AWS, but also uses other cloud providers in case of an AWS outage. After an AWS outage in April 2011, he noted that the organization had no significant downtime "because of the redundancy we built into the application architecture."[60]

Effective access controls and backups are essential for the protection of an organization's data. They are also essential for the protection of the organization itself, because they will ensure that the company can effectively address questions brought during legal actions, such as a lawsuit or a government investigation.

Compliance and Risk

As organizations rely more and more on digital data, legislators around the world have worked to protect the rights and privacy of individuals whose sensitive information exists on computers. For example, the American Health Insurance Portability and Accountability Act (HIPAA) of 1996 holds the health care industry to stringent regulations about patient histories and treatment records.

Private health information may be placed at risk by the use of mobile and personal devices in health-care settings.

Consequently, organizations that are subject to HIPAA regulations and that wish to move to the cloud need to ensure that the provider can meet specific demands of encryption and recovery.

However, even the most diligent company can be subject to data security issues. Many businesses are adopting the practice called Bring Your Own Device (BYOD) in which employees are permitted and even encouraged to use their favorite laptop, tablet, or smartphone at work, on the road, and at home. This means employees can access sensitive information from locations around the world. These portable devices become targets for thieves. Some criminals are interested only in the device's potential for resale; others target specific individuals because of who their employer is and the potential of accessing sensitive information. Other types of incidents are possible when individuals make mistakes. For example, in January 2013, a health care provider employee failed to comply with company and state health department regulations when she downloaded sensitive patient information onto a USB drive, which she then lost. Some six thousand patient identification records were compromised. The employee was fired.

Individuals' safety and privacy may also be put at risk through the use of cloud-based platforms, such as social media sites. Oversharing information such as home addresses or phone numbers can lead to embarrassing questions of who is responsible and why the action occurred. One example of oversharing with unexpected consequences took place in Canada. In June 2012, Diane Glenn's teenage son invited three friends to his house in Barrie, Ontario, for a small party. When one of the guests put the host's address on Twitter, the evening quickly got out of hand. Eventually, more than two hundred teenagers showed up; according to one account, "Some revelers stole jewelry and prescription drugs, while others broke cabinets and stair posts. By the end of the night, the partiers had caused an estimated $40,000 in damage."[61]

Financial Cloud Precautions

The fracas in Barrie was started by one tweet, most likely from a mobile phone, sent to the cloud, where it spread far beyond expectations. The incident also exposed the Glenn family to the danger of identity theft. The teenage thieves may have been interested only in the contents of the prescription drug containers, but in the wrong hands, the information on the containers can put a patient's health records at risk. Identity theft could also occur if the family's sensitive financial records were stolen. Modern cloud-based paperless Internet banking reduces this risk, but only if proper precautions are taken by both the customer and the financial institution.

Customers engaging in cloud-based banking need to take a number of precautions. The most fundamental of these are using an effective password, safeguarding the password, and ensuring that they access their information in a safe location away from prying eyes. The banking institution, on the other hand, has much greater risk. Inadequate software protections and encryption can lead to hackers accessing account information. Large-scale attacks by thousands of computers working to breach an institution's security, called distributed denial of service (DDoS) attacks, can cause the targeted system to reset or overload and, in some circumstances, fail. As businesses move to cloud-based servers, they may become vulnerable to such assaults. For example, Australian security firm Arbor Networks noted in a study released in January 2013 that 94 percent of that nation's data centers were regularly subjected to DDoS episodes, and just over a third had suffered firewall failures as a result.

These incidents occur around the world. A series of DDoS actions against many of the largest banks in the United States, including Wells Fargo, Bank of America, and PNC in late 2012 and early 2013 resulted in temporarily reduced or halted services. According to the *New York Times,* although no money was stolen, these attacks represented something new:

Security researchers say that instead of exploiting individual computers, the attackers engineered networks of computers in data centers, transforming the online

HOW A DISTRIBUTED DENIAL OF SERVICE (DDOS) AND OTHER HACKER ATTACKS WORK

An attacker infects a computer after gaining access using a virus or phishing tactics. The infected computer in turn connects with other computers that can also be controlled by the attacker. In a DDoS attack, thousands of computers may be used to overwhelm the victims' servers with data requests. Slave computers also spread spam, malware, and viruses to infect new computers.

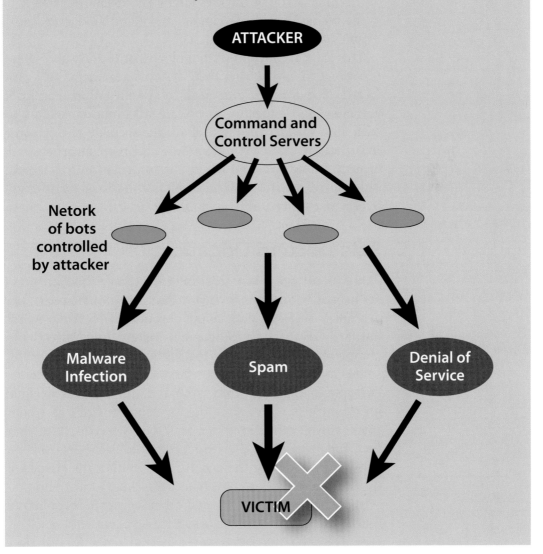

equivalent of a few yapping Chihuahuas into a pack of fire-breathing Godzillas. . . . By using data centers, the attackers are simply keeping up with the times. Companies and consumers are increasingly conducting their business over large-scale "clouds" of hundreds, even thousands, of networked computer servers. . . . It appears the hackers remotely hijacked some of these clouds and used the computing power to take down American banking sites. "There's a sense now that attackers are crafting their own private clouds," either by creating networks of individual machines or by stealing resources wholesale from poorly maintained corporate clouds, said John Kindervag, an analyst at Forrester Research.[62]

This new trend obliges financial institutions and cloud providers to ensure that their systems are adequately protected. Not doing so may lead to system failures, security breaches, and exposure of private information, which, in turn, may lead to questions about the security of electronic information. Affected individuals and their attorneys will want to know how and where the information was stored. This raises questions about which court has jurisdiction over a case of data in the cloud.

Relevance to Litigation

Large cloud providers distribute customer data on servers in many locations to ensure effective global access. For example, AWS has data centers around the world, including facilities in Japan, Singapore, Ireland, and Australia to complement its centers in the United States. Additionally, some cloud vendors may not serve as the actual host to the customer's data. Attorney Wahab notes, "When a cloud user contracts with a provider, . . . that provider may contract with another provider for cloud services, who may then turn around and contract for cloud services from yet another provider, to the point where neither the client nor the original provider know where the client's information is actually being stored."[63] He and other legal experts point out that a negotiated clause in a service-level agreement (SLA) can ensure that the data is stored in a particular jurisdiction.

A comprehensive SLA should also clarify the legal standing of the data being stored. According to Wahab, "For any business, it is imperative that the SLA clearly state that the client retains all ownership in the data it stores with the provider. This is especially important if the organization plans to store any copyrighted, trademarked, or patented content,"[64] which would include such protected content as music, video, artwork, or manuscripts. The SLA must also cover potential litigation. A court-issued subpoena compels an organization to turn over requested electronic data, whether it is located on an in-house server or in the cloud. Wahab's associate Lauren Mack notes that the SLA "should also address how both parties will respond to subpoenas or discovery requests and who will bear the costs associated with producing the requested data,"[65] and how quickly the provider must produce the data.

Sometimes, however, the owner of the data is not aware that law enforcement agencies are in touch with the cloud provider. In some jurisdictions, cloud-based data can be accessed without the permission of the data's owner.

Examining and Seizing Cloud-Based Data

The proliferation of electronic data for both legal and illegal purposes has led lawmakers to enable law enforcement agencies to examine such data for evidence of illegal activity such as terrorism. For example, in the United States, the USA PATRIOT Act allows the U.S. government to seize information stored in the United States, or that is accessible from the United States, without informing the parties involved. The government is also not required to give the parties an opportunity to contest the intrusion. As Mack observes, "This ability may conflict with privacy laws concerning the private data of [a business's] customers who live outside the US."[66]

Private individuals outside the United States may be subject to such action as well. A report to the European Parliament in January 2013 contends that American law enforcement agencies and courts may use the U.S. Foreign Intelligence and Surveillance Amendments Act to compel American companies doing business in Europe to hand over data about Europeans. The report accuses the United States of directing "heavy-caliber mass surveillance firepower aimed at the cloud,"[67] and warns that Europeans are at risk of having personal information from Facebook, Google, and Microsoft exposed.

Even without dealing with questions of surveillance or terrorism, attorney Ashish S. Prasad points out that the courts "may consider information stored on the cloud, including private social networking information, to be discoverable," meaning that it may be subject to inclusion in a court case. He says, "Courts have indicated that information relating to social media may be relevant to litigation. Courts have recognized that information contained in a person's Facebook account, for example, could be subject to discovery in litigation"[68] and ultimately allowed in a court case.

Social Cloud in Court

Electronic records have some similarities to traditional written records that are used in everyday court cases. Like written records, they can be misplaced, stolen, and accidently or deliberately destroyed. Unlike written records, they can be difficult to examine in court because they may be irretrievable due to variety of computer problems, such as a hard drive failure, or they may only exist in an outmoded format. From a legal standpoint, this presents a challenging question of whether or not electronic records can be used in court. According to Prasad, "the technology has been outpacing the revision of existing rules and regulations."[69] In the absence of such revisions, court decisions have varied about whether or not cloud-based information is admissible in court. For example, Federal Rule 34(a) (1) compels individuals or organizations to provide documents and electronically stored information within a party's possession,

custody, or control. This would certainly pertain to an in-house server or data center, but may not pertain to information stored in the cloud; while the data might not be in the party's direct custody or possession, it might be interpreted by a court as being in the party's control.

Cloud-based social media information may fall under this rule as well. Prasad comments that while some decisions have upheld the privacy of social media profiles or messages, the trend in case law "suggests that individuals' private postings through social media sites will not be afforded a great deal of privacy protection by the courts."[70] He cites a decision in which a court concluded that because a site such as Facebook could access all user posts, and because the site's terms of service allow it to disseminate the postings when it was deemed appropriate, even a posting marked private could not be expected to be fully confidential.

Social media profiles and messages are not the only expressions of personal thoughts and opinions that today are sent to and from the cloud. Debates over the status of cloud-based e-mails and text messages continue to occur across

Cloud-based social media information, such as Facebook posts, may be considered admissible in court in some circumstances.

the United States, as courts and legislators work to reconcile technology with the law.

"A Reasonable Expectation of Privacy"

Court decisions about other messages in the cloud present a collage of contradictory rulings. In some cases, courts have ruled that personal e-mails in the cloud accessed via a work computer are admissible because of where they were read; in other cases, such messages were deemed inadmissible unless they have an impact on the business or its reputation. The privacy of text messages also varies. For example, courts in Florida and Georgia have ruled that law enforcement may search an individual's cell phone for relevant evidence without a warrant or subpoena, while courts in Ohio and Rhode Island have ruled that such messages are private unless subject to a search warrant. Rhode Island Superior Court associate justice Judith Savage wrote that "people have a reasonable expectation of privacy in the contents of their text messages with no distinction between whether the messages were sent or received by them."[71]

In the same decision, Savage recognized the questions regarding technology and the law, saying, "Even the United States Supreme Court has struggled with the legal

In some U.S. jurisdictions, police may search cell phones and read text messages without a warrant or subpoena.

challenges raised by emerging technology, most especially in the realm of cellular phones and their contents,"[72] deferring to the lower courts to interpret the laws of the land.

In such an atmosphere, law enforcement officials and other interested parties are hoping that federal legislation can clarify the status of electronic communications in their investigations and prosecutions. In December 2012, representatives from law enforcement agencies spoke during hearings by the U.S. Senate related to updating the 1986 Electronic Communications Privacy Act to recognize current cloud technology. One of the provisions they wanted included in updated legislation would require cellular telephone providers to record and store information about subscribers' text messages for two years. This would represent a huge amount of data; estimates show Americans send roughly 6 billion texts daily from mobile devices.

The changing interpretations of what electronic data is subject to law enforcement investigation and to courtroom discovery has helped give rise to an emerging field of cloud computing. In keeping with the previous labels, this one is another "aaS."

Security-as-a-Service

One of the growing sectors of cloud computing involves third-party providers offering "Security-as-a-Service," or "SecaaS." These cloud-based services can be deployed on either in-house or cloud infrastructures, making them useful for organizations running all types of cloud models. SecaaS provides a variety of customizable controls to perform such tasks as filtering e-mail, controlling access to outside websites such as social media outlets, and providing adjustable log-in access. SecaaS providers such as Symplified, Actiance, and OneLogin provide managers with the ability to limit or expand access when necessary. This can be particularly useful when dealing with individuals who need to have temporary access to a company network, such as vendors or health care providers. The service enables the user to see who has logged on and when, and can be deployed across multiple devices and platforms.

Cloud Washing

Individuals and organizations looking to move their important data to the cloud need to do some homework before taking the leap. One of the unfortunate trends associated with the rise of cloud computing is a practice called cloud washing. The term applies to companies that advertise cloud services that are not actually cloud-based. According to technology writer Margaret Rouse:

> As the cloud computing delivery model becomes more popular and the uses for cloud services expand, so will the number of vendors hoping to present their offerings as having a cloud feature or function. Cloud washing has been compared to green washing, the rebranding of products and services as being friendly to the environment. In both instances, though, "wash" means to apply a thin layer of paint to freshen something up and make it look new. The paint, in this case, is a marketing message.[1]

The key to avoiding cloud washing is research. A true cloud computing provider will offer self-service setup, elastic addition and subtraction of virtual servers, a pay-as-you-go model, and much more. Otherwise, the company may be offering a traditional server hosting environment.

1. Margaret Rouse. "Cloud Washing." SearchCloudStorage, August 2011. http://searchcloudstorage.techtarget.com/definition/cloud-washing.

Research firm Gartner predicts demand for SecaaS will continue to grow as more businesses move to the cloud, with spending reaching $4.2 billion by 2016. Gartner's Eric Ahlm believes, "Demand remains high from buyers looking to cloud-based security services to address a lack of staff or skills, reduce costs, or comply with security regulations quickly."[73]

However, SecaaS may not be the appropriate permanent solution for every organization. Some organizations are committed to ensuring their own employees have the most up-to-date security skills. They prefer to work with the nonprofit CSA. Working with affiliates across the computing industry, CSA offers a way to ensure that a company's IT staff can gain proficiency in cloud security.

Proficiency and Certification

CSA promotes cloud computing best practices through research and education. Educational opportunities include webinars and training sessions held in locations worldwide. Recognizing that cloud computing security has a lack of industry standards, CSA developed a two-level proficiency course toward a Certificate of Cloud Security Knowledge. The certification is an industry first, providing a basic and an advanced course of training for professionals responsible for cloud computing.

The training begins with an in-depth discussion of the cloud before moving to recommendations from national and international security organizations. Hands-on activities enable participants to bring a fictional company securely into the cloud. CSA notes that this training does not replace certifications in other areas of IT, which may be required by employers; instead, the training is designed to augment previously obtained credentials in order to "help individuals better cope with the increasingly pervasive cloud computing issues they are now facing."[74]

CSA hopes this certification program will enable professionals to gain a greater understanding of cloud computing and help organizations move forward while growing the cloud. Jerry Archer, chief security officer of education for financial services company Sallie Mae, believes that the program will help in "setting the bar" for professionals and organizations associated with cloud security. He says CSA "is challenging security practitioners to become the cloud thought leaders we need today and tomorrow to ensure safe and secure cloud environments."[75]

This leadership will likely be necessary in the coming years. All indications are that cloud computing is here to stay.

CHAPTER 5

Clouds on Every Horizon

Cloud computing continues to grow. Individuals and organizations are communicating and collaborating through cloud-based e-mail, presentations, videos, and more. Thanks to the cloud, entrepreneurs can run their businesses and students can work on school projects from adjacent tables in the same coffeehouse. The entrepreneur can check inventory and sales contacts, approve payroll entries, or add more storage capacity to a cloud server due to a spike in website traffic, all from a laptop. The student can edit a video for a presentation, collaborate with other students in a school across town or across the ocean, or check homework assignments, all from a tablet. This demonstrates the increasing growth of the cloud in everyday life.

Growth in All Directions

The cloud continues to gain supporters among providers and customers alike. In early 2013, North Bridge Venture Partners, with help from GigaOM Research, began its third annual Future of Cloud Computing poll. They received replies from 855 people at 57 technology companies, including well-known players such as Microsoft, Amazon Web Services (AWS), and Rackspace and lesser-known companies with cloud-centric names such as Cloudability and CloudBees. North Bridge invests in emerging fields of technology, including the cloud. Consequently, the firm has an interest in where the technology is headed. In June, it released the poll's results.

The numbers revealed that cloud computing continues to grow, with 75 percent of participants using some sort of cloud platform; this number was up from 67 percent in the 2012 survey. The growth occurs on each layer of "the stack," with IaaS leading the charge, with a 29 percent increase of deployment over 2012. However, PaaS may have the greatest expansion ahead; 33 percent of respondents said they were using it, a 22 percent increase from 2012, but 72 percent of survey participants said they expected to deploy some type of PaaS in the next five years.

An interesting result concerns the use and future of hybrid cloud models. Currently, the adoption of public and private clouds is roughly equivalent, with public clouds having a slight lead over private ones. However, those numbers are forecast to change in the next five years. More than three-quarters of the respondents said they expect hybrid cloud models to be at the heart of their cloud strategies going forward. Sameer Dholakia, group vice president and general manager of the Cloud Platforms Group at cloud provider Citrix, believes the hybrid model is the wave of the future: "The ideal end-state for businesses is a flexible hybrid cloud strategy where IT is able to aggregate and deliver self-service access to a variety of cloud services, both internal and 3rd party, and run these workloads on any cloud that best fits the service."[76]

According to Michael J. Skok, North Bridge general partner, this continued expansion "is consistent with forecasts from GigaOM research, which expects the total worldwide . . . market for cloud computing to reach $158.8 B[illion] by 2014, an increase of 126.5 percent from 2011."[77] These numbers clearly reflect confidence in the cloud.

"Cloud Computing Just Isn't as Scary as It Once Was"

Skok also believes that the overall results of the poll forecast a continued confidence in cloud computing. He says that while "we are still very early in the cloud-computing revolution," overall cloud adoption and enthusiasm "are clearly on an unstoppable rise."[78] For those who participated in the North Bridge poll, scalability, flexibility, and cost continue to be the leading reasons for switching to the cloud, as they have been throughout the short history of the poll.

Following the 2012 poll, author Joe McKendrick wrote in Forbes.com, "Cloud computing just isn't as scary as it once was to companies and their CIOs."[79] The 2013 numbers reflect that the present-day adoption of the cloud is continuing to be driven by such adventurous businesspeople. More than half of the respondents reported using applications that advance business priorities, such as file sharing, CRM, and collaboration.

On the other hand, the cloud's most robust future may lie in IT applications, as the participants felt that IT areas such as mobile apps, backup, and security will generate tremendous growth. These areas are part of the larger predictions of global expansion of cloud technologies in the coming years. Research firm Gartner predicted in mid-2012 that cloud computing will grow by more than 100 percent to become a $207 billion industry by 2016. Information technology analysis firm IDC predicted that business revenues related to cloud innovations will top $1 trillion by 2020. Driving these numbers are investments in cloud provider infrastructures.

Expanding Infrastructure

Cloud providers are expanding their infrastructure in order to meet the predicted future demands. For example, Google spent $1.2 billion in the first three months of 2013 on expanding its data centers around the world. This expenditure included $600 million to expand its data center in Lenoir, North Carolina, and $390 million to expand a data center in

Belgium. Their investment continued into the spring; on April 23, they announced a $400 million expansion of its data center in Council Bluffs, Iowa. Interestingly, on the same day, Facebook said that it planned to construct a data center in Altoona, Iowa; the first phase of the construction would cost $300 million, and the center would come online in 2014.

GigaOM's Stacey Higginbotham wrote that "the dueling news releases . . . highlight a growing infrastructure rivalry between these web giants."[80] Microsoft also announced expansion plans less than a month later. It publicized plans for data centers in the Australian states of New South Wales and Victoria, making it easier for Australian users of its Azure cloud services to store their data within their own country. Additionally, Microsoft released plans for a center in Singapore, joining Amazon, Salesforce, and IBM in the small country.

Google, Facebook, and Microsoft may attract a lot of public attention with their announcements, but the leader in global data centers is a hosting company called Equinix. It has two centers in Singapore, along with more than ninety other centers in fifteen countries across five continents. They provide cloud platform services for businesses across a variety of industries, including finance and entertainment. Their strategy of placing data centers around the world enables them to compete with the more well-known names in cloud hosting. But such competition comes at a cost.

The Cost of Competition

Data center expansion is a competitive field. As the largest companies grow in competition with each other, it is difficult for smaller companies to enter the field. John Engates, chief technical officer of Rackspace, observes that trying to create a new cloud data center provider "is very expensive,"[81] and any new startup would need to have a

<aside>
BITS & BYTES
$1.2 billion
Amount spent by Google to expand its worldwide data centers from January through March 2013.
</aside>

Cloud Storage Price Competition

In November 2012, cloud storage providers Amazon Web Services (AWS) and Google engaged in a weeklong price competition in an attempt to increase business.

On November 26, as AWS was preparing to hold its inaugural cloud conference, Google announced it was reducing its price on standard storage by more than 20 percent. When the conference began two days later on November 28, Amazon announced price reductions of up to 27 percent. AWS senior vice president Andy Jassy noted that this was not the first time that AWS had cut its prices, saying, "We've lowered prices 23 times since 2006."[1] The following day, November 29, Google followed up by cutting its prices a further 10 percent.

Analysts surmised that Google was attempting to lure customers away from AWS, the cloud storage leader. Barb Darrow, GigaOM technology writer, wrote on November 26, "Announcements like this one should at least give pause to people who doubt that Google is serious about providing cloud infrastructure services for business users."[2] On November 29, she wrote, "Clearly, the game is on,"[3] as Google tried to compete with AWS. But her sentiment of the whole affair might have snuck through in the title of the article: "Ok, This Is Getting Silly: Google Cuts Storage Prices—Again."

1. Quoted in Larry Dignan. "Amazon Web Services Cuts S3 Prices, Knocks Old Guard Rivals." Between the Lines (blog), ZDNet, November 28, 2012. www.zdnet.com/amazon-web-services-cuts-s3-prices-knocks-old-guard-rivals-7000008039.

2. Barb Darrow. "Google Spiffs Up Its Cloud—Tale That Amazon!" GigaOM, November 26, 2012. http://gigaom.com/2012/11/26/google-spiffs-up-its-cloud-take-that-amazon.

3. Barb Darrow. "Ok, This Is Getting Silly: Google Cuts Storage Prices—Again." GigaOM, November 29, 2012. http://gigaom.com/2012/11/29/ok-this-is-getting-silly-google-cuts-storage-prices-again.

minimum of 100,000 square feet (30,500 sq. m) of space. By comparison, the $300 million first phase of Facebook's new Altoona, Iowa center will be more than 400,000 square feet (122,000 sq. m).

Some well-established businesses have tried to compete in cloud services without success. ZDNet's Jack Clark notes that domain hosting company GoDaddy "shutdown its cloud service a year after launching it."[82] Other businesses have decided that the best way to take advantage of the growth of the cloud is to develop partnerships with large cloud providers. For example, in March 2012, IaaS provider Eucalyptus Systems reached an agreement with Amazon Web Services, which today allows their customers to use specialized APIs to work in both Eucalyptus and AWS environments. Developers test their software through Eucalyptus to ensure that it works as planned in the AWS environment. For example, a Eucalyptus customer called AppDynamics tests new software for Netflix, AWS's largest customer. Thomas Morse, the director of information technology and operations at AppDynamics, says, "Even before their software is on AWS, we are categorizing over a billion transactions. Netflix inflicts a unique kind of pain on a system, with tens of thousands of computing nodes supporting millions of actions a minute."[83]

Eucalyptus was established as an open-source company through which organizations could build private clouds, but investigated working with AWS as Amazon's own cloud services expanded. Marten Mickos, CEO of Eucalyptus, noted that "They've got hundreds of thousands of customers now," and because each customer is a company, AWS "is used by millions of people. . . . Amazon is the standard now."[84]

By mid-2013, AWS had nearly seven hundred such partnerships. At the same time, its website listed more than one thousand job openings in their global facilities, from software development engineers in Luxembourg and South Africa to sales managers in Hong Kong and Australia. IDC predicts that by 2017, spending on public and private clouds will create nearly 14 million jobs worldwide—of which 1.2 million will be in the United States and Canada. Analysts wonder if there will be enough trained individuals to meet the demand.

"It Took Us Around Six Months to Recruit All of Them"

The projected growth of cloud computing in the coming years will be a challenge to information technology professionals. According to the U.S. Bureau of Labor Statistics, the traditional segment of IT is expected to grow no more than 3 percent per year through 2020. However, the cloud computing segment is forecasted to expand much more rapidly;

Chennai, India, is home to dozens of IT business parks, including the campus of Tata Consultancy Services, which provides computer services, including cloud-based offerings, to companies worldwide.

one study from IDC, sponsored by Microsoft, projects such growth as 26 percent per year through 2015.

Currently, the demand is outstripping the supply. In 2012, nearly 2 million IT jobs went unfilled because applicants lacked the necessary cloud-related skills. AMP Technologies, a startup in Chennai, India, discovered this shortage firsthand as they tried to build their cloud in 2012. Rujuta Rammohan, head of AMP's human resources department, said that it was extremely difficult to hire fifteen employees with the specific cloud computing skills they needed. She said, "It took us around six months to recruit all of them."[85]

The IDC study suggests a two-pronged approach to this shortage of qualified personnel. Firstly, retrain existing IT professionals, and secondly, encourage students to acquire cloud-related skills and certifications. To that end, Microsoft and Amazon are offering relevant programs. Microsoft Learning's programs deal with the cloud in general. Its self-paced Virtual Academy is designed for IT professionals to gain new skills, and its online IT Academy is designed for those looking to enter the workforce. Lutz Ziob, Microsoft Learning's general manager, says, "Our goal is to continue to prepare the existing workforce and students for the jobs of tomorrow and empower them to develop their skills"[86] for the years ahead. Amazon's training program takes a different approach, concentrating on its own cloud structure. Its classroom-based AWS Certification Program is designed to create proficiency in the AWS suite. Its website says the goal is to enable individuals to gain "the technical skills and knowledge associated with best practices for building secure and reliable cloud-based applications using AWS technology."[87]

The need for retraining and certification may account for reluctance surrounding adopting the cloud, but it is only one inhibiting factor. A reluctance to adopt a new technology often involves more than just unfamiliarity with it.

Cloud Inhibitors

A significant inhibiting factor in adopting cloud technology may be more rooted in psychology than technology. Keiran Conboy, a senior lecturer at National University of Ireland Galway, believes that among IT managers "there may be unfounded fears of eventual downsizing even though higher productivity as a result of the cloud can boost company prospects and job security."[88] The 2013 North Bridge Ventures poll results may bear that out, depending on personal perspective. The poll's results showed that 47 percent of respondents who had adopted the cloud reported that doing so had led to current or future reductions in IT personnel. On the other hand, some respondents painted a rosier picture: 34 percent felt adopting the cloud had no effect on their IT staffing levels, and 19 percent said it would lead or has led to new hiring.

A further apprehension about the cloud—one that is both technological and psychological—lies in the area of security. The North Bridge Ventures study found that 46 percent of the participants felt cloud security was a significant concern. This reflected an 18 percent drop from the 2012

Upgrade APIs to Combat Cyberattacks

Imagine a company that manages pensions or retirement plans tied to the stock market. In order to better serve its customers, it creates a mobile app. A customer uses the app to access current market information via the firm's application programming interfaces (API), and may do so several times a day. However, during a denial-of-service attack, an automated system directs the app to call the API thousands of times a second. The API becomes overwhelmed as it tries to handle the attack, restricting or denying access by legitimate users. It might even be disabled.

Security expert Mark O'Neill believes that API attacks are the next battleground for denial-of-service attacks. He says:

> As mobile app penetration and usage grows, and bank customers use apps as their main channel to perform banking transactions, the impact an API attack can have on an economy grows exponentially. Customers are unable to pay bills, transfer money, or ensure they have funds to make purchases.[1]

The key to securing the API is to separate its security from that of the website. An emerging field of programming called API management works to detect and block unusual access-request patterns, and secure access through enhanced identification levels.

1. Mark O'Neill, "Cloud APIs—The Next Battleground for Denial-of-Service Attacks," Cloud Security Alliance, April 13, 2013. https://blog.cloudsecurityalliance.org/2013/04/13/cloud-apis-the-next-battleground-for-denial-of-service-attacks.

poll, but Skok still labels it the "top inhibitor"[89] to cloud adoption. Andrew Jaquith, chief technical officer and senior vice president for cloud strategy at cloud security provider SilverSky, says, "Security concerns continue to be the number one barrier to adoption of cloud services. This isn't surprising: companies are understandably reluctant to move sensitive data and business functions to the cloud when they don't understand the cloud provider's capabilities."[90] Skok is nonetheless confident that these concerns will diminish over time. "If you look back to the late [19]90s, people said they'd never use their credit cards on the Internet to buy things. Well, look what happened there."[91]

The poll listed the ability to comply with regulations as the second-highest concern, followed by apprehensions over privacy and over vendor lock-in, in which a company may discover its cloud-based data cannot be easily retrieved from a provider because it has been stored in a format used only by that provider. An interesting result was that the perceived cost of moving to the cloud and provider cost were judged among the least-inhibiting factors. However, as the cloud becomes the standard form of doing business, costs and regulations could go hand-in-hand. Legislators across the United States are already beginning to regulate and to tax what happens in the cloud.

Multiple Clouds in Different Locations

The development of cloud computing technology has led a number of U.S. state legislators to take crash courses in the cloud. In 2012, a legislative study committee of the Vermont State Legislature invited the head of the University of Vermont's computer science department to present an introduction to cloud computing before they could debate whether sales in the cloud should be regulated or taxed—similar to sales tax collected on business software sold at an office supply store. The committee also heard from a representative of Washington's Department of Revenue, who noted that his state taxes remotely accessed software in the same way it taxes a song that is purchased online.

Currently, Vermont does not collect sales tax on cloud purchases. Other states, such as Pennsylvania and Utah, collect sales tax on software that is remotely accessed by a state resident. A third set of states, including Virginia and Rhode Island, has made cloud computing sales nontaxable because no tangible personal property is transferred in the transaction. In other words, since there is no box containing a music CD or software program, it is not subject to tax.

"Without the Cloud, We Simply Couldn't Afford to Start Up"

Organizations both old and young are discovering the advantages of the cloud. Andrew Montalenti is the chief technology officer at Parse.ly, which has provided web traffic analyses to online publishers since 2009. He said, "The alternative [to the cloud] is you have to get a $5 million investment just to buy your servers. And then you find out no one wants your product anyway, so now you have wasted all this money on servers."[1] Garry Prior helped create Taxi for Two in 2012, which enables travelers to share cabs in London, England. He declared, "Without the ability to run our infrastructure on the cloud, we simply couldn't afford to start up."[2]

But the cloud works for established enterprises as well. NASA used the cloud to create websites dedicated to the landing and the mission of the Mars rover *Curiosity*. Additionally, the British charity Action for Children, founded in 1869, moved to the cloud to keep up with public interest and demand for its resources. They placed their website and other portions of their business in a public-private hybrid cloud, which enables them to analyze data from social media to create more efficient fundraising and to keep sensitive information in-house but accessible to staff members away from the office.

1. Quoted in Brian Nicholson, Ali Owrak, and Lucy Daly. "The Economic Impact of the Cloud on UK Businesses." Rackspace.com and Manchester Business School White Paper, n.d. www.rackspace.co.uk/white papers.

2. Quote in Rackspace.com. "88 Per Cent of Cloud Users Point to Cost Savings According to Rackspace Survey." *The Rackspace Blog! and Newsroom*, February 20, 2013. www.rackspace.com/blog/newsarticles/88-per-cent-of -cloud-users-point-to-cost-savings-according-to-rack space-survey.

However, future legislative sessions in these and other states may amend or overturn these interpretations as cloud-based business becomes more commonplace.

The current jumble of regulatory questions will become even more muddled as more data becomes stored in internationally based centers. Some jurisdictions have already addressed this possibility. For example, Canadians who bank with companies that also do business across the border in the United States must, by law, be told that their personal information may be stored in the United States and that data may be subject to the laws where it is stored. Stuart Hargreaves, a professor at Toronto's York University Osgoode Hall Law School, says, "The biggest complication is probably figuring out exactly which laws apply to the data you are storing in the cloud. Cloud servers can in theory be located anywhere in the world, but cloud providers are not always clear on exactly which of their data centers will be hosting your data—in fact, it could be in multiple centers, in different locations."[92]

As overseas data centers come online, the concept of granularity will become more widespread. In this aspect of cloud computing, companies develop data centers in specific geographic locations for customers in that area, so that the customers are assured that their data complies with local and national regulations. This will reduce the confusion noted by financial analyst Patricia Hines. She says that such regulatory questions are particularly prevalent in the Asia-Pacific region, which includes countries such as Japan, South Korea, China, Singapore, and Australia. She says that her company's Asian customers "seek the benefits offered by cloud computing to expand their geographic reach and product suites, but struggle with interpreting the disparate regulations, laws and guidelines being issued across the region."[93] New granular data centers can help Hines' clients and others continue to shape how they do business overseas.

"They All of a Sudden Get to Say 'Yes'"

The Internet has helped international business grow, and cloud computing is making it easier for these firms to conduct business around the world. As Internet connectivity grows, businesspeople, students, and ordinary citizens can access cloud services anywhere they can reach the web. Such access has fueled the expansion of the practice of Bring Your Own Device (BYOD), enabling employees to read their e-mail and access important documents both at home and on the road.

Cloud computing is also transforming how people work behind the scenes. IT professionals may no longer need to manage their own servers, but they will still need to manage the virtual infrastructure of their company's clouds. They also have the opportunity to try new ideas and gain new skills. Paul Keen is the technology and development manager at RedBalloon, an online gift card retailer based in Sydney, Australia. His company uses AWS for its clouds, and he notes that the cloud means his IT staff are "working with developers much more closely, so they can potentially do programming work or make sure they're . . . being proactive . . . to see if there are any problems" before they impact the business. He says his staff enjoys the changes because they get to be creative "instead of just dealing with hardware."[94]

AWS vice president Adam Selipsky believes that the cloud will help change the reputation of IT departments as "the people that say no":

> We've seen time and time again that developers, system administrators, architects, find that using the cloud is really a freeing or a liberating experience, where they all of a sudden get to say "yes."
>
> They get to say, yeah, we can provision new resources for you very quickly, very easily, very low cost. . . . They're going to be concerned with managing those environments in a highly scalable, highly automated fashion.
>
> And then, importantly, managing the applications that sit on top of that infrastructure. And at the end of the day that sort of task will provide more value to the enterprises than the more traditional sort of tasks [of IT].[95]

The traditional tasks of the IT department are not the only areas of the workplace that are being reshaped by the expansion of cloud computing. It has started to transform entire industries.

Transformations

The expansion of the cloud into mainstream business and everyday life is challenging a variety of occupations beyond information technology and those who work directly with the infrastructure. As with any technological upheaval,

individuals in a number of fields will need to acquire new skills to adapt to the transforming landscape.

Retailing, advertising, and marketing are already undergoing significant changes. Individuals accustomed to using cloud-based services, such as Pandora or Netflix, represent a growing segment of the population. Cutting-edge and cloud-savvy advertisers create and marketers sell commercials, short videos, and animated advertising to catch users' attention. The next generation of ads will target individuals based on their streaming habits. Sales staff will no longer need to travel to make presentations, as cloud-based meeting applications such as GoToMeeting or Adobe Connect allow salespeople to interact with clients and share video demonstrations of their latest products. As Christopher Barnatt puts it, "The more we cloud compute, the more we will therefore be able to take planes out of the sky and vehicles off the road."[96] For those occasions when personal

Microsoft employees demonstrate the Live Meeting videoconference service on a Chicago, Illinois, elevated train platform in 2003. A number of newer, cloud-based conferencing services continue to give consumers the ability to hold meetings anywhere.

visits are necessary, the cloud-enabled employee can keep in touch with the office through a smartphone or tablet, accessing necessary information directly from the cloud.

The media and publishing industries are also being transformed. Traditional broadcasting through television and radio is being augmented or replaced by cloud-based streaming through applications such as Roku, Hulu, or Amazon Prime. Traditional print media, including newspapers, books, and magazines, are working to reach Internet-enabled readers by adapting their offerings to tablets and e-readers such as the Kindle.

Moreover, any individual involved in customer service must understand the role that effective cloud-based social media strategies play in shaping opinion and driving consumer patterns. Communicating with customers is no longer confined to advertising on radio, television, or on a website. Customer feedback in the cloud takes the form of viral YouTube videos or trending Twitter hashtags, reaching millions of users. Enthusiasts can instantly help shape opinions about a new film, musical performance, or electronic device, and they can do so from their workplace, their home, or their classroom.

Accelerated Education Interest

The cloud offers tremendous potential for enhancing education environments both inside and outside the traditional classroom. Schools are adopting BYOD policies or are creating a noncompetitive environment through a practice called one-to-one, in which every student works with the same type of device. Schools are also expanding programs called blended learning, which combines traditional educator-moderated learning with online content and instruction.

The adoption of these practices is moving quickly. Each year, the New Media Consortium (NMC) issues a report that identifies current and coming trends in education. They place the trends in time-to-adoption timeframes of one year or less, two to three years, and four to five years. The 2010 *NMC Horizon Report* noted that "Cloud computing, viewed in 2009 as two to three years away from mainstream adoption, has seen dramatic uptake by schools over the past twelve months."[97] Subsequent reports noted that schools were replacing in-house e-mail and backup systems with cloud-based services. They also noted that educators were bringing into the classrooms online collaborative tools, including the Google Docs and Microsoft 365 suites of programs, and multimedia apps such as Splashup or SlideShare. They also mentioned that teachers were expanding the use of cloud-accessing tablets, mobile devices, and apps. The 2013 report noted that cloud computing was again a hot topic as "the impact of this technology continues to unfold in new and expanding ways. Its rapid integration into our everyday lives—from technology infrastructure, to communication exchanges, to the many apps and resources used for informal learning—has only accelerated institutional interest in cloud computing."[98] It highlighted such cutting-edge uses of the cloud, referring to a school district in Wisconsin that is creating video-based curricula for online distance learning, and a suburban Washington, D.C. high school that is partnering with aerospace firm Northrup Grumman to develop an interactive cloud to access science, technology, engineering, and mathematics resources.

The NMC also studies trends in higher education and demonstrates that trends and technologies that enter college classrooms eventually find their way into K-12 environments. For example, they envision that by 2016, college classrooms will feature game-based learning to foster collaboration and team-building through simulations and role-playing games. These future classrooms will also feature augmented reality capabilities that will combine 3-D modeling with cloud-based apps to investigate topics that are difficult to experience firsthand, such as overseas landscapes or internal anatomy. A further potential classroom trend is called the Internet of Things, in which small cloud-connected objects are placed on almost anything. They can provide preprogrammed information such as temperature, humidity, or location, and classroom applications include using them on plants in a biology classroom or on remote outdoor locations to track weather conditions.

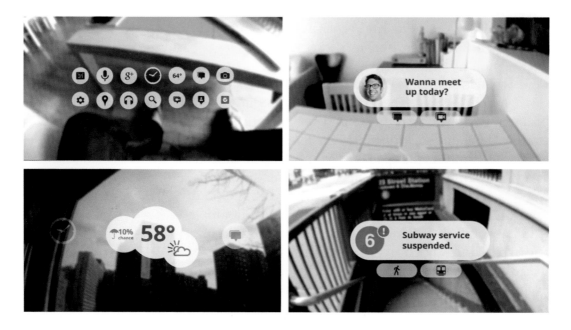

An image created by the team behind Google Glass shows how its potential application of Internet of Things technology might look.

The Internet of Things also includes online data from the thousands of surveillance cameras that watch roads, buildings, and more, enabling anyone to observe traffic patterns in cities around the world. All of this data needs to be stored somewhere, and the cloud provides the most efficient means of doing so.

Consolidating into a Government Cloud

Internet-connected devices, gadgets, cameras, and more are combining to bring the cloud further into the everyday experience. The U.S. government recognizes that the cloud offers significant potential for improving its services to American citizens. To that end, the government is working to streamline many of its public and research information capabilities through increased use of cloud computing.

The U.S. government's Data Center Consolidation Task Force seeks to save taxpayers' dollars by reducing the number of servers and data centers the federal government operates nationwide and to consolidate their information to cloud-based operations. The task force hopes to close twelve hundred of the nearly twenty-nine hundred data centers

Inside a Government Cloud Initiative

The United Kingdom is working to move government IT operations to the cloud. Their initiative, called Government Cloud Computing (G-Cloud), is focused on the cloud's ability to reduce costs and increase flexibility and efficiency when delivering public services.

Within the initiative is an online marketplace called CloudStore, where SMBs can advertise their services in order to compete for government contracts. Over 70 percent of the suppliers on G-Cloud are SMBs, and offer SaaS, PaaS, and IaaS in public, private, and hybrid cloud models. According to CloudStore lead Mark Craddock, these SMBs can offer better value than some traditional government vendors. He says, "One government department went out to [an IT consultant for a job] and was quoted £4 million [$6.2 million]. When it went to G-Cloud, it was quoted £50,000 [$77,000]."[1]

Suppliers in CloudStore must meet a variety of government standards such as completely documenting the costs of their services, where the customer's data will be stored, and how the data will be returned at the end of the contract. They must also provide an additional layer of protection for their government clients. But these restrictions have not dampened the popularity of CloudStore. As of May 2013, more than eight hundred suppliers were enrolled, advertising more than seven thousand types of cloud services.

1. Quoted in Bill Goodwin, "CW500: Inside the government's CloudStore," *ComputerWeekly.com*, November 2012. www.computerweekly.com/feature/CW500-Insidethe-governments-CloudStore.

by the end of 2015. Their efforts are bearing fruit nationwide. Its May 2013 progress report itemized more than one thousand centers that were already closed or were scheduled for closing. For example, the Department of Energy's Los Alamos National Laboratory decommissioned one hundred physical servers in a data center and moved the data to three hundred virtual machines on thirteen physical servers. The result was faster and more flexible computing power for data processing and storing, with a savings of $1.4 million in current infrastructure costs.

Moving to the cloud also saves the government valuable tax dollars in the future. Current operating expenses will be shifted to payments for on-demand cloud services. Capital expenditure (CapEx) and operating expenses (OpEx) for future data centers are eliminated. The overall consolidation effort will also bring further savings to the U.S. government. Industry analyst Jason Verge, writing for *Data Center Knowledge,* notes, "The plan aims to bring $3 billion in savings, but there are varying predictions. [Office of Management and Budget] predictions range from $3 billion to $5 billion. In a GAO report, agencies predicted around $2.4 billion in savings."[99] One of the significant cost savings will be in energy consumption, as older data centers are consolidated to newer and more energy-efficient locations. Additionally, many cloud providers are working to reduce energy consumption and lessen their impact on the environment.

Is the Cloud Green?

Computers of all sizes run on electricity, either directly or via rechargeable batteries. Data centers alone currently account for as much as 2 percent of global electricity use. That figure would only increase as more traditional data centers come online. All of this leads to more pollutants and greenhouse gases in the atmosphere from electricity-generating factories. Several companies, including Apple, Facebook, and Google are trying to reduce the cloud's impact on the environment by taking advantage of renewable and alternative energy sources to help power their newest data centers. For example, Apple created a solar panel array covering nearly 100 acres (40ha) at its Maiden, North Carolina, data center to provide 60 percent of the facility's electricity. Google and Facebook will be using electricity from local wind farms to help power their facilities in Iowa.

Google has also determined that they can reduce their energy consumption by raising the temperatures inside their server rooms. Traditionally, these spaces have been air-conditioned to protect sensitive electronics. However, Google discovered that their servers could withstand much higher temperatures than expected; consequently, they raised their server areas from 68°F (20°C) to approximately

80°F (27°C). They also pioneered a method of capturing the excess heat in the server rooms. The hot air rises from the servers to heat water in coils above the rooms; the warm water is then pumped through outdoor radiators to dissipate the heat, and then recirculated inside. In an October 2012 interview with *CBS This Morning,* Google's senior vice president Urs Hölze said, "We're estimating that we saved over a billion dollars in the history of Google through these efficiency measures."[100]

Google's measures represent one company's efforts to ensure that their part of the cloud is as green as possible. The company also helped fund a study by the U.S. Department of Energy's Lawrence Berkeley National Laboratory and Northwestern University's McCormick School of Engineering to assess the future environmental impact of the cloud. The study estimates that if the entire U.S. business community moved just three basic computing tasks (e-mail, CRM functions, and productivity programs such as word processing, spreadsheets, and presentation and collaboration tools) to the cloud, annual energy savings would be 23 billion kilowatt-hours, or enough "to meet the annual electricity needs of Los Angeles, the nation's second largest city."[101]

A Google employee checks the solar energy panels on one of company's buildings. The use of alternative energy sources is only one of the strategies used by computer data companies to improve their impact on the environment.

Greening the Cloud

Data centers run by cloud services providers require large amounts of electricity to run the servers, the heating and cooling, the security systems, and much more. This electricity may be generated by power plants burning fossil fuels, thus possibly contributing to worldwide climate change. One cloud provider is working to change that model.

GreenQloud is based in Iceland and offers IaaS modules including compute, network, and storage resources. It has partnerships with software, platform, and database vendors to provide SaaS and PaaS services as well. The company also notes that its services are also compatible with Amazon Web Services products.

What makes GreenQloud different from other cloud services providers is that it runs its servers completely on renewable energy sources. Seventy percent of its electricity comes from hydroelectric generators and 30 percent comes from geothermal energy. GreenQloud customers can track how much energy they use through the provider and can determine the amount of pollutants they are keeping out of the atmosphere due to GreenQloud's renewable energy model.

Clearly, the cloud computing industry is not fully green, but few global industries can support that claim. However, recent advances in alternative energy sources and in data center efficiencies may help drive the industry forward toward a greener future. And if some predictions come true, it will be a future filled with screens.

"We'll Simply Do Whatever We Do"

Many computer users already have more than one device accessing the Internet. Screens on tablets, laptops, smartphones, and televisions all can access cloud content. Tim Bajarin, president of the technology analysis firm Creative Strategies, Inc., believes that this is just the beginning. He surmises that, "Within the next three to five years, we will make a dramatic move from personal to personalized computing." The devices we use now will represent just a few of the screens available. "Over time, we'll see a whole crop of new screens emerge that will tie us each to our personal cloud to make personal computing truly personalized."[102] He also predicts wearable screens will move beyond the Google Glass eyewear project, to include flexible glass devices that resemble wristwatches or bracelets that can access personal clouds.

Certainly, the Internet is making more and more information available to worldwide users every day that they can move to their personal clouds. But the key to effectively using these personalized clouds today and tomorrow is to understand that there needs to be a mix of what we store in our clouds and what we store in our heads. Education experts and psychologists note that thinking skills need to exist independently from factual knowledge. Annie Murphy Paul, a journalist and consultant who studies how we learn, says:

> Just because you can Google the date of Black Tuesday doesn't mean you understand why the Great Depression happened or how it compares to the recent economic slump. There is no doubt that the students of today, and the workers of tomorrow, will need to innovate, collaborate and evaluate . . . but such skills can't be separated from the knowledge that gives rise to them. To innovate, you have to know what came before. To collaborate, you have to contribute knowledge to the joint venture, and to evaluate, you have to compare new information against knowledge you've already mastered.[103]

The cloud computing revolution is in full swing. Businesses, schools, organizations, and individuals are discovering the cloud's potential for communication, collaboration, and innovation. It is helping individuals around the world learn about new ideas and points of view, and they, in turn, are helping to move the cloud forward into additional aspects of everyday life. In so doing, the technology becomes more commonplace and more accepted. Industry insiders Cary Landis and Dan Blacharski believe that the future's "cloud desktop" will probably "look a lot like today's PC desktop. The underlying technologies will be different, but we'll leave those details to the techies. Soon, the hype will subside, but the cloud will be here to stay. We will use it without thinking about it. We'll simply log on to do whatever we do."[104]

Chapter 1: From Mainframes to Servers

1. Jim Meigs. "Inside the Future: How PopMech Predicted the Next 110 Years." *Popular Mechanics,* December 10, 2012. www.popularmechanics.com/technology/engineering/news/inside-the-future-how-popmech-predicted-the-next-110-years-14831802.

2. Meigs. "Inside the Future."

3. Tim Berners-Lee with Mark Fischetti. *Weaving the Web: The Original Design and Ultimate Destiny of the World Wide Web by Its Inventor.* New York: HarperCollins, 1999, pp. 33–34.

4. Andy Reinhardt. "Iomega's Zip Drives Need a Bit More Zip." *Business Week,* August 12, 1996. www.businessweek.com/1996/33/b3488114.htm.

5. Quoted in Ed Sperling. "Next-Generation Data Centers." *Forbes,* March 15, 2010. www.forbes.com/2010/03/12/cloud-computing-ibm-technology-cio-network-data-centers_3.html.

6. Quoted in Sperling. "Next-Generation Data Centers."

7. Quoted in Sperling. "Next-Generation Data Centers."

8. Quoted in "Government of Canada to Reduce Information Technology Costs and Save Taxpayers' Dollars." Canada News Centre, August 4, 2011. http://news.gc.ca/web/article-en.do?nid=614499.

9. Neha Prakash. "Did You Know That Cloud Computing Has Been Around Since the '50s?" Mashable, October 26, 2012. http://mashable.com/2012/10/26/cloud-history.

10. Jessi Hempel. "Is Pinterest the Next Facebook?" *Fortune,* March 22, 2012. http://tech.fortune.cnn.com/2012/03/22pinterest-silberman-photo-sharing.

11. Quoted in "Pinterest on AWS-Customer Success Story." Amazon Web Services, June 4, 2012. http://youtube.com/watch?v=KGpXhFOu4y4.

12. Quoted in Quentin Hardy. "Active in Cloud, Amazon Reshapes Computing." *New York Times,* August 27, 2012, p. A1. wwwnytimes.com/2012/08/28/technology/active-in-cloud-amazon-reshapes-computing.html?_r=0.

Chapter 2: "The Stack": SaaS, IaaS, and PaaS

13. Quoted in Brian Fonseca. "Technology Innovators: Dave Moellenhoff." *InfoWorld,* March 4, 2002, p. 52.

14. Fonseca. "Technology Innovators: Dave Moellenhoff."

15. "Software as a Service: Strategic Backgrounder." Software and Information Industry Association, 2000, p. 4. www.siia.net/estore/ssb-01.pdf.

16. Ben Kepes. "Cloud U: Understanding the Cloud Computing Stack: SaaS, PaaS

and IaaS." Rackspacehosting, March 19, 2012. http://youtube.com/watch?v=RN5sg5Lnyy8.

17. Quoted in Asha Nayaka. "Lineup SaaS Solutions Goes Live at Hackney Citizen." Lineup.com News and Information, Dec. 19, 2012. www.lineup.com/news/lineup-saas-solutions-goes-live-at-hackney-citizen.

18. Quoted in Workday. "Workday and Brown University: A Unified Approach Brings New Insight." 2012. www.workday.com/Documents/pdf/case-studies/workday-brown-university-case-study.pdf.

19. Ben Kepes. "Say Goodbye to DIY Data Centers." Rackspace Knowledge Center, September 12, 2012. www.rackspace.com/knowledge_center/whitepaper/cloudu-series-say-goodbye-to-diy-datacenters.

20. Quoted in Kepes. "Say Goodbye to DIY Data Centers."

21. Kepes. "Say Goodbye to DIY Data Centers."

22. Kepes. "Say Goodbye to DIY Data Centers."

23. Christopher Barnatt. *A Brief Guide to Cloud Computing: An Essential Guide to the Next Computing Revolution.* London, UK: Robinson, 2010, p. 96.

24. Kepes. "Cloud U: Understanding the Cloud Computing Stack."

25. ActiveState Software Inc. "Private PaaS 101: What It Is and Why You Need It." 2012, p. 4. www.activestate.com/sites/default/files/pdfwp/whitepaper-private-paas-101.pdf.

26. Sanjay Srivastava. "How to Convince Your CEO About PaaS' Benefits." GMO Cloud America, December 4, 2012. https://us.gmocloud.com/blog/2012/12/04/how-to-convince-your-ceo-about-paas-benefits.

27. Ben Kepes. Tech podcast. April 29, 2013.

Chapter 3: The Social Cloud

28. Mary Phillips-Sandy. "Kenneth Cole's Egypt Tweet Offends Just About Everyone on Twitter." AOL News, February 3, 2011. www.aolnews.com/2011/02/03/kenneth-coles-egypt-tweet-offends-just-about-everyone-on-twitte.

29. Quoted in CNN.com. "Internet Goes Wild over 'Binders Full of Women.'" October 16, 2012. http://politicalticker.blogs.cnn.com/2012/10/16/binders-full-of-women-trending.

30. Quoted in Chris Morran. "Waitress Who Posted No-Tip Receipt from 'Pastor' Customer Fired from Job," *The Consumerist,* January 31, 2013. http://consumerist.com/2013/01/31/waitress-who-posted-no-tip-receipt-from-pastor-customer-fired-from-job.

31. Quoted in Herb Weisbaum. "Applebee's Social Media Faux Pas a 'Learning Experience.'" Nbcnews.com, February 5, 2013. www.nbcnews.com/business/applebees-social-media-faux-pas-learning-experience-1B8251556.

32. Quoted in Weisbaum. "Applebee's Social Media Faux Pas."

33. Quoted in Weisbaum. "Applebee's Social Media Faux Pas."

34. Quoted in Weisbaum. "Applebee's Social Media Faux Pas."

35. Quoted in Tonia Ries. "Gatwick Airport to Publish New Children's Stories Via SoundCloud." *Reatime Report,* July 25, 2012. http://therealtimereport.com/2012/07/25/gatwick-airport-to-publish-new-childrens-stories-via-soundcloud.

36. Manual Roig-Franzia. "Internet Radio Royalty: Debate of Artists' Pay Goes Through Pandora's Founder." *Washington Post,* April 4, 2013, p. C-9.

37. John-Scott Dixon. "Music in the Cloud." *Cloud Magazine,* May 24, 2012.

http://thecloudmagazine.com/music-in-the-cloud.

38. Rocky Mountain Mike. Personal correspondence. May 14, 2013.

39. Quoted in Jane L. Levere. "In-Room Entertainment Turns Away from TV." *New York Times,* April 30, 2013, p. F2. www.nytimes.com/2013/05/01/business/hotel-guests-turn-away-from-tv-and-toward-streaming-media.html?pagewanted=all&_r=0.

40. Quoted in Brad Howarth. "Game Developers Look to the Cloud." *Sydney Morning Herald,* December 4, 2012. www.smh.com.au/it-pro/cloud/games-developers-look-to-the-cloud-20121204-2aru4.html.

41. Quoted in Erik Kain. "EA Turns Its Back on Single-Player Games, Embraces the Cloud." *Forbes,* September 6, 2012. www.forbes.com/sites/erikkain/2012/09/06/ea-turns-its-back-on-single-player-games-embraces-the-cloud.

42. Quoted in Margo Pierce. "Cloud Storage in the Real World." *THE Journal,* October 3, 2012. http://thejournal.com/articles/2012/10/03/cloud-storage-in-the-real-world.aspx?=THECL.

43. Quoted in Carmen McCollum. "Middle School Using Cloud Computing for Down-to-Earth Education." Hobart Community.com, September 18, 2012. www.nwitimes.com/news/local/lake/hobart/middle-school-using-cloud-computing-for-down-to-earth-education/article_377a141f-b5f7-56e9-b3af-8dd408781e13.html.

44. Dian Schaffhauser. "Windows Azure (Finally) Takes Infrastructure into Cloud." *THE Journal,* April 16, 2013. http://thejournal.com/Articles/2013/04/16/Windows-Azure-Finally-Takes-Infrastructure-into-Cloud.aspx?Page=2.

Chapter 4: Downtime and Security in the Cloud

45. Quoted in Brian X. Chen. "'The Cloud' Challenges Amazon." *New York Times,* December 26, 2012. www.nytimes.com/2012/12/27/technology/latest-netflix-disruption-highlights-challenges-of-cloud-computing.html.

46. Quoted in Chen. "'The Cloud' Challenges Amazon."

47. Barb Darrow. "Christmas Eve AWS Outage Stings Netflix but Not Amazon Prime." GigaOM.com, December 25, 2012. http://gigaom.com/2012/12/25/christmas-eve-aws-outage-stings-netflix-but-not-amazon-prime.

48. David Linthicum. "Calculating the True Cost of Cloud Outages." InfoWorld.com, February 8, 2013. www.infoworld.com/d/cloud-computing/calculating-the-true-cost-of-cloud-outages-212253.

49. John Omwamba. "Cloud Security: Fears and Challenges." CloudTweaks, August 28, 2012. www.cloudtweaks.com/2012/08/cloud-security-fears-and-challenges.

50. Quoted in David Geer. "7 Deadly Sins of Cloud Computing." CSO Online, January 2, 2013. www.csoonline.com/article/725101/7-deadly-sins-of-cloud-computing?page=2.

51. Quoted in Amit Chowdhry. "How the NASA Curiosity Mars Rover Used the Amazon Cloud." Pulse 2.0, August 11, 2012. pulse2com/2012/08/11/how-the-nasa-curiosity-mars-rover-used-the-amazon-cloud.

52. Chowdhry. "How the NASA Curiosity Mars Rover Used the Amazon Cloud."

53. Quoted in Andrea Chang. "NASA Uses Amazon's Cloud Computing in Mars Landing Mission." *Los Angeles Times,* August 9, 2012. http://articles.latimes.com/2012/aug/09/business/la

-fi-tn-amazon-nasa-mars-20120808.

54. Office of Inspector General. "NASA's Progress in Adopting Cloud-Computing Technologies." General Accounting Office, July 29, 2013, p. iii. http://oig.nasa.gov/audits/reports/FY13/IG-13-021.pdf.

55. Kaiser Wahab. "Cloud Service Contracts: Breaking Down the All Important Service Level Agreement (SLA)." *Security Advocate,* March 20, 2013. www.thesecurityadvocate.com/2013/03/20/cloud-service-contracts-breaking-down-the-all-important-service-level-agreement-sla.

56. Quoted in Geer. "7 Deadly Sins of Cloud Computing."

57. Quoted in Mary Brandel. "Cloud Security: the Basics." CSO Online, June 15, 2010. www.csoonline.com/article/596819/cloud-security-the-basics.

58. Quoted in Brandel. "Cloud Security: the Basics."

59. Quoted in Brandel. "Cloud Security: the Basics."

60. Quoted in Bob Violino. "Amazon Outage a Valuable Lesson in Cloud Security." CSO Online, April 28, 2011. www.csoonline.com/article/680894/amazon-outage-a-valuable-lesson-in-cloud-security.

61. CTV News, "Twitter Post Draws Hundreds to Crash Barrie, Ont. House Party." June 26, 2012. www.ctvnews.ca/canada/twitter-post-draws-hundreds-to-crash-barrie-ont-house-party-1.854081.

62. Nicole Perlroth and Quentin Hardy. "Bank Hacking Was the Work of Iranians, Officials Say." *New York Times,* January 8, 2013, p. B1.

63. Wahab. "Cloud Service Contracts."

64. Wahab. "Cloud Service Contracts."

65. Lauren Mack. "Top Questions to Ask Before Your Business Stores Company Data in the Cloud." *Security Advocate,*

May 13, 2013. www.thesecurityadvocate.com/2013/05/13/top-questions-to-ask-before-your-business-stores-company-data-in-the-cloud.

66. Mack. "Top Questions to Ask Before Your Business Stores Company Data in the Cloud."

67. Didier Bigo, Gertjan Boulet, Caspar Bowden, Sergio Carrera, Julien Jeandesboz, and Amandine Scherrer. "Fighting Cyber Crime and Protecting Privacy in the Cloud." Directorate-General for Internal Policies, Policy Department C: Citizens' Rights and Constitutional Affairs, p. 35. www.europarl.europa.eu/committees/en/studiesdownload.html?languageDocument=EN&file=79050.

68. Ashish S. Prasad. "Cloud Computing and Social Media: Electronic Discovery Considerations and Best Practices." Metropolitan Corporate Counsel, February 2012, p. 26. www.metrocorpcounsel.com/pdf/2012/February/26.pdf.

69. Prasad. "Cloud Computing and Social Media."

70. Prasad. "Cloud Computing and Social Media."

71. Judith Savage, Superior Court, State of Rhode Island and Providence Plantations. *State of Rhode Island v. Michael Patino.* September 4, 2012, p. 188. http://statecasefiles.justia.com/documents/rhode-island/superior-court/10-1155.pdf?ts=1347031354.

72. Savage. *State of Rhode Island v. Michael Patino,* p. 44.

73. Quoted in Sam Shead. "Security-as-a-Service Captures the Eyes of the Enterprise," ZDNet, April 16, 2013. www.zdnet.com/security-as-a-service-captures-the-eyes-of-the-enterprise-7000014022.

74. Cloud Security Alliance. "Cloud Security Alliance CCSK Certification FAQ."

2013. https://cloudsecurityalliance.org /wp-content/uploads/2013/02/CCSK -V3-FAQ.pdf.

75. Quoted in "Certificate of Cloud Security Knowledge: What the Industry Says." Cloud Security Alliance, 2013. https://cloudsecurityalliance.org/edu cation/ccsk.

Chapter 5: Clouds on Every Horizon

76. Quoted in Slide 31. "2013 Future of Cloud Computing 3rd Annual Survey Results." May 29, 2013. www.slide share.net/mjskok/2013-future-of -cloud-computing-3rd-annual-survey -results.

77. Michael J. Skok. "2013 Future of Cloud Computing 3rd Annual Survey Results." June 19, 2013. www.entre capitalist.com/resource/2013-future -cloud-computing-3rd-annual -survey-results.

78. Skok. "2013 Future of Cloud Computing 3rd Annual Survey Results."

79. Joe McKendrick. "Cloud Computing Simply Isn't That Scary Anymore: Survey," Forbes.com, June 20, 2012. www .forbes.com/sites/joemckendrick/2012 /06/20/cloud-computing-simply-isnt -that-scary-anymore-survey.

80. Stacey Higginbotham. "Data Center Rivals Facebook and Google Pump $700M in New Construction into Iowa." GigaOM, April 23, 2013. http:// gigaom.com/2013/04/23/data-center -rivals-facebook-and-google-pump -700m-in-new-construction-into -iowa.

81. Quoted in Jack Clark. "IT's New Battlegrounds in the Cloud Revolution." ZDNet, November 15, 2012. www.zd net.com/its-new-battlegrounds-in-the -cloud-revolution-7000006902.

82. Clark. "IT's New Battlegrounds."

83. Quoted in Quentin Hardy. "Amazon's Boom in Cloud Partners." New York Times, April 29, 2013. http://bits.blogs .nytimes.com/2013/04/29/amazons -boom-in-cloud-partners.

84. Quoted in Hardy. "Amazon's Boom in Cloud Partners."

85. Quoted in Ishan Srivastava. "Cloud Computing: Only 5% Techies are Job-Ready," Times of India, December 21, 2012. http://articles.timesofindia.india times.com/2012-12-21/internet /35952764_1_cloud-and-mobility -workforce-hcl-technologies.

86. Quoted in Jennifer LeClaire. "Need Work? Learn Cloud Computing: 7 Mil Jobs by 2015." Sci-Tech Today, December 24, 2012. www.sci-tech-to day.com/news/Cloud-Ready-IT-Jobs -Up-26--Yearly/story.xhtml?story_id =12000DEF9N60&full_skip=1.

87. Amazon Web Services. "AWS Certification Program Overview." 2013. http://aws.amazon.com/certification.

88. Quoted in "Psychological and Social Factors May be Critical in Implementing Cloud Computing." Lero—The Irish Software Engineering Research Centre, January 16, 2013. www.lero.ie /news/psychologicalsocialfactorswell technologymaybecriticalimplementing cloudcomputing.

89. Skok. "2013 Future of Cloud Computing 3rd Annual Survey Results."

90. Quoted in Slide 45. "2013 Future of Cloud Computing 3rd Annual Survey Results." June 19, 2013.

91. Quoted in Barb Darrow. "Enterprises to Cloud: Ready or Not, Here We Come." GigaOM, June 20, 2012. http:// gigaom.com/2012/06/20/enterprise-to -cloud-ready-or-not-here-we-come.

92. Quoted in Christine Dobby. "Offshore Data Storage Clouds Security Picture," Financial Post, November 21, 2012. http://business.financialpost.com/2012

/11/21/offshore-data-storage-clouds
-security-picture/?__lsa=3d44-6cc5.

93. Patricia Hines. "Sibos 2012: The Impact of Regulation on Cloud Computing." Finextra, November 21, 2012. www.finextra.com/Community/Full Blog.aspx?blogid=7156.

94. Quoted in Rohan Pearce. "How Cloud Is Reinventing the IT Department." *Computerworld,* May 1, 2013. www.computerworld.com.au/article /460627/how_cloud_reinventing_it _department.

95. Quoted in Pearce. "How Cloud Is Reinventing the IT Department."

96. Barnatt. *A Brief Guide to Cloud Computing,* p. 20.

97. New Media Consortium. "The 2010 Horizon Report: K-12 Edition," p. 6. www.nmc.org/system/files/pubs /1316814904/2010-Horizon-Report -K12.pdf.

98. New Media Consortium. "Horizon Report: 2013 K-12 Edition," p. 11. www .nmc.org/pdf/2013-horizon-report -k12.pdf.

99. Jason Verge. "U.S. Government Closes 64 More Data Centers." Data Center Knowledge, November 27, 2012. www .datacenterknowledge.com/archives /2012/11/27/hows-the-federal-data -center-consolidation-plan-going.

100. Quoted in "Behind the Cloud: A Tour of Google's Secretive Data Facilities." *CBS This Morning,* October 17, 2012. www.cbsnews.com/8301 -505263_162-57533989/behind-the -cloud-a-tour-of-googles-secretive -data-facilities.

101. Eric Masanet, Arman Shehabi, Lavanya Ramakrishnan, Jiaqi Liang, Xiaohui Ma, Benjamin Walker, Valerie Hendrix, and Pradeep Mantha. "The Energy Efficiency Potential of Cloud-Based Software: A U.S. Case Study." Lawrence Berkeley National Laboratory, 2013, p. 16. http://crd.lbl .gov/assets/pubs_presos/ACS/cloud _efficiency_study.pdf.

102. Tim Bajarin. "The Future of Personal Computing: Cloud-Connected Screens Everywhere." *Time,* August 13, 2012. http://techland.time .com/2012/08/13/the-future-of-perso nal-computing-cloud-connected -screens-everywhere.

103. Annie Murphy Paul. "We Still Need Information Stored in Our Heads Not 'in the Cloud.'" *Time,* June 21, 2013. http://ideas.time.com/2013/06/21/we -still-need-information-stored-in -our-heads-not-in-the-cloud.

104. Cary Landis and Dan Blacharski. *Cloud Computing Made Easy,* p. 65. www.cloudipedia.com/wp-content /uploads/2009/11/cloud_computing _made_easy.pdf.

GLOSSARY

API: The abbreviation for application programming interface. An API is a type of software that enables computer programs to communicate without user input.

CapEx: The abbreviation for capital expenditure, which refers to the initial, upfront payment for a particular piece of equipment, such as a server, or for a service, such as a contract with a cloud computing provider.

cloud: The descriptive term for information that computer users can access via the World Wide Web without the need for purchasing and installing specialized programs on their computers.

cloud computing: Technology that enables consumers, developers, and businesses to communicate and collaborate by accessing software applications, data storage, and computing processing capacity over the Internet.

CRM: The abbreviation for customer relationship management. CRM programs enable companies to organize and automate sales, marketing, customer service, and technical support.

data center: A purpose-built structure that houses a collection of computer servers and associated resources dedicated to the storage and retrieval of information.

DDoS: The initialism for distributed denial of service. Coordinated attacks by sometimes thousands of computers, directed at a single company, in order to test and/or breach its security.

dumb terminal: In the early days of computing, a dumb terminal connected the user from a remote location to the mainframe.

granularity: In cloud computing, a model in which data centers or clouds are specifically designed/located to serve a specific group of customers. For example, a data center located in Canada that hosts only Canadian customers and information is a granular facility.

hypervisor: The term for a set of hardware and software connected directly to a computer's storage disks. Installing a hypervisor on a server enables the computer to run multiple independent copies of operating systems.

IaaS: The abbreviation for Infrastructure-as-a-Service. IaaS refers to the foundation of the cloud-based server stack upon which a computer developer can construct a system to meet a particular need.

instance: The term for a copy of an operating system that can be installed on a hypervisor to enable virtualization.

mainframe: In the early days of computing, a mainframe served as a centralized computer to which various users connected via separate terminals. See also dumb terminal.

microblog: A site that allows users to share thoughts and comments in a cloud-based social media setting, such as Twitter or Tumblr.

OpEx: The abbreviation for operating expense. An OpEx is a recurring—and often predictable—cost such as the rent associated with equipment, office space, or cloud provider services.

OS: The abbreviation for operating system. In computers, an operating system is the software that enables the hardware to perform particular tasks. Popular operating systems include Windows, Macintosh, and Linux.

PaaS: The abbreviation for Platform-as-a-Service. PaaS is the middle layer of the cloud computing stack and serves as a platform for the creation of software delivered via the web.

SaaS: The abbreviation for Software-as-a-Service. SaaS is the top layer of the cloud computing stack in which software programs are delivered via the Internet without the need for download or installation.

SecaaS: The abbreviation for Security-as-a-Service. An emerging field of cloud computing in which customizable security measures can be applied to a company's infrastructure.

server: The term for a computer with expanded memory capacity that works as a centralized storage unit.

SLA: The initialism for service-level agreement. An SLA is an important negotiated contract between a cloud provider and a customer.

SMB: The initialism for small to mid-size business. SMB is a catchall phrase that includes any commercial operation that is not a large corporate enterprise.

the stack: The term for the levels of cloud computing, including SaaS, PaaS, and IaaS.

virtualization: One of the technological innovations that make cloud computing possible. Virtualization separates the operating system from the underlying hardware, enabling data center servers to be available for a myriad of uses.

VPN: The abbreviation for virtual private network, in which a series of servers are connected to the Internet for a particular business or organization and are accessible only by permission.

FOR MORE INFORMATION

Books

Christopher Barnatt. *A Brief Guide to Cloud Computing: An Essential Guide to the Next Computing Revolution*. London: Robinson, 2010. Lecturer and futurist Barnatt shares a variety of insights about cloud computing, its origins, its current state, and its future, in an easy-to-read conversational style.

David Crookes. *Cloud Computing in Easy Steps*. Leamington Spa, UK: Easy Steps Limited, 2012. This illustrated book presents step-by-step tips for some of the cloud's most popular programs, including Google Apps, Apple iCloud, Flickr, and more.

Cary Landis and Dan Blacharski. *Cloud Computing Made Easy*. Cloudipedia.com, 2013. Industry veterans Landis and Blacharski present a concise guide to the cloud, including their top ten misconceptions about cloud computing.

Barrie Sosinsky. *Cloud Computing Bible*. Indianapolis: Wiley, 2011. Sosinsky provides a comprehensive overview of many of the features of cloud computing and the services associated with it, including those from Google and Amazon.

Fred van der Molen. *Get Ready for Cloud Computing*. Zaltbommel, Netherlands: Van Haren, 2010. Part I provides a concise guide to cloud computing and virtualization. Part II shares perspectives from industry experts working with leading IT vendors in the cloud computing field. Part III provides in-depth examples of how several organizations moved to the cloud.

Websites

CloudTweaks (www.cloudtweaks.com). This website covers a wide range of cloud-related topics, including jobs, startups, and informative graphics that summarize trends and developments. The "Cloud Humor" section provides a different look at the cloud.

ExplainingComputers.com—Cloud Computing (www.explainingcomputers.com/cloud.html). Developed by lecturer and futurist Christopher Barnatt, this site provides a guide to many aspects of computing, with the "Cloud Computing" page being of particular interest.

INDEX

Electronic record legal issues, 88–90
E-mail
    computer firm development, 17
    court-based legal decisions, 90
    employee lessons, implementation, 20
    Google Apps integration, 26, 33, 71
    management by servers, 23, 25
    SaaS advantages, 37
    SecaaS integration, 91
    server inaccessibility issues, 74
    VPN integration, 73

F

Facebook, 54–58, 60, 63, 67–68, 88–89, 97, 112
Floppy disks, 19, *19*
Foursquare, 75

G

Game-based learning, 109
Google Android operating system, 39, 57
Google Apps, 29, 71, 81
Google Docs, *9,* 40, 109
Google Gmail, 26, 33
Google Maps, 59
Google+, 55
GoToMeeting, 107

H

Hacker attacks, 84, *85,* 86
Hashtags, 55–57, *56,* 108
Hybrid cloud model, 43, *46,* 53, 95, 104, 111

I

iCloud service, 29
Infrastructure-as-a-Service (IaaS), 40–46, 48–53, *50,* 72–73, 80–81, 111, 114
iTunes, 62–63

K

Kays, Jonathan, 11

L

Laptop computers, 13, 37, 66, 71, 83, 94, 114

M

Mainframe computers, 13, 14–18, 22
Microblogging, 54–57
Microsoft
    cloud computing, 29–30, 59, 77, 94
    data centers, 97
    gaming and, 68
    IaaS and, 45, 73
    personal computing, 39
    security, 88
    service outages, 75
Microsoft Azure, 51
Microsoft Learning program, 100–101
Movies/TV streaming services, 65, *66*
Music-streaming services, 62–63

N

Netflix, 65–66, 75, 99, 107
New Media Consortium (NMC) report, 108–109

P

Pinterest, 30–31, *31,* 55, 75
Platform-as-a-Service (PaaS), 48–53, *50,* 80–81, 95, 111, 114
PlayStation 4, 69, *69*
Private cloud model, *46,* 47, 86, 95, 99
Public cloud model, *46,* 47, 77, 95

S

Security concerns
    access and backups, 79–82

PICTURE CREDITS

ABOUT THE AUTHOR

Andrew A. Kling has relied upon the cloud to stay in touch with friends, family, and business contacts, and to back up his computers, since 2000. He is a webmaster and newsletter editor, as well as a freelance author, consultant, and bookseller. He enjoys history, hockey, travel, music, good books, and spending time with his wife, Laurie, and their famous Norwegian Forest cat, Chester.